Stories from African-Caribbean-Canadian Seniors in the Region of Peel

Edited by
ANGELA J CARTER

Suite 300 - 990 Fort St
Victoria, BC, V8V 3K2
Canada

www.friesenpress.com

First Edition — 2019

This book was made possible through a grant from the Government of Canada's New Horizon for Seniors Program.

ISBN
978-1-5255-4841-3 (Hardcover)
978-1-5255-4842-0 (Paperback)
978-1-5255-4843-7 (eBook)

1. BIOGRAPHY & AUTOBIOGRAPHY, CULTURAL HERITAGE

Distributed to the trade by The Ingram Book Company

Table of Contents

Preface

The idea for this book was born when members of the Healthy, Active & Wise Seniors group of the United Achievers' Community Services Inc. (UACS)* were gathered around a table at one of their regular meetings. The majority of the members were from the Caribbean, and they were reminiscing about growing up in their various countries of birth and reflecting on how different their childhood was from that of their children and grandchildren who were born or raised in Canada. The stories were so rich in content and in lessons learned through experience that it was proposed we should capture those stories to pass on to current and future generations.

It took a couple of years to develop and prepare this book, with a few stumbling blocks along the way, but now here it is!

We have featured 38 stories in this book but there are so many more to capture. We hope that we – or others – will continue to capture the stories of immigrants to Canada, who had to fight prejudice, bigotry and racism, and dispel the myths about people from the Caribbean and Africa.

You will read voices in the first person and in the third person – as that's how they chose to tell their stories.

We believe that those who read this book will have a better understanding of the contributions that immigrants have made and continue to make to this country they call home. Through these stories and others to follow, we hope that you will be touched by the perseverance and resilience of people who wanted to give their best no matter their circumstances.

We welcome your feedback and comments.

Angela J Carter
Editor & Executive Director, RootsCS

**During the publishing stages of this book, our organization went through a restructuring process, resulting in a name change from United Achievers' Community Services Inc.to Roots Community Services Inc. (RootsCS). This name and concept better reflect our mission and vision, and the communities we serve.*

Acknowledgements

It took a combined effort to produce this book. Apart from the storytellers whose stories are included in the book, there were the behind-the-scenes teams, including members of the Healthy, Active & Wise Seniors of the United Achievers' Community Services Inc. (UACS), college students who were completing their placements at UACS, professionals, and volunteers.

Almost everyone involved was an amateur to book publishing, but each eagerly rose to the occasion, learning how to conduct interviews, take photographs, transcribe tapes, and write stories. Therefore, we take this opportunity to acknowledge those who have helped to bring this project to fruition. They are:

Project Coordinators

- Grace Newsome
- Izierin Ohiro

Healthy, Active & Wise Seniors

- Dorothy Cornelius
- Lorna Cushnie

Victoria Fraser
William West

Placement Students
Gertrude Baffour
Carine Cox
Yvana Robin
Abisola Taiwo

Volunteers
Sandra Cushnie
Rachel Oluwo
Davene Leslie

Consultants
Natalie Francis
Rhona Lindo

Many thanks to all of you for your contribution. We especially give thanks to the Government of Canada's Employment and Social Development Canada division for funding this project through the New Horizon for Seniors Program.

We know that this book will be a blessing to many.

Angela J Carter
Executive Director, RootsCS

Caribbean Immigration to Canada

"November 3rd, 1955, will be a memorable day and year for our group in Canada, and one which I hope will be remembered in the future with delight, for it was on this day that a group of 18 girls, the vanguard of 100 selected girls from Barbados and Jamaica, entered Canada as immigrants in a special arrangement between the Governments of Jamaica and Barbados and the Canadian Department of Labour."[1] This is an excerpt from a report written by Donald Willard Moore, president of the Negro Citizenship Association, on the arrival of the first group of women from the Caribbean who immigrated to Canada under the newly established West Indian Domestic Scheme.

This was indeed a memorable day, because just over a year earlier, on April 27, 1954, Donald Moore had led a delegation

1 This is an excerpt from a report written by Donald Moore entitled "Director's report on the occasion of welcoming to Canada the first contingent of 100 Negro immigrant girls from Barbados and Jamaica, Montreal, November 3, 1955."

of Black individuals and supporters to Ottawa to present a brief to the then Minister of Citizenship and Immigration, Walter E. Harris, that protested the "discriminatory and dangerous" immigration policies.[2] This remarkable event was the first time a Black-led delegation embarked on such a journey.

At that time, the immigration policies defined British subjects as "by birth or by naturalization in the United Kingdom, Australia, New Zealand, or the Union of South Africa, and citizens of Ireland." As noted in the brief, "This definition excludes from the category of British Subjects those who are in all other senses British subjects but who come from such areas as the British West Indies, Bermuda, British Guiana, Ceylon, India, Pakistan, Africa, etc."[3]

Another "official reason" that was being used to restrict non-white immigration was that people from tropical areas "will have great difficulty in adjusting themselves to the Canadian climate." This myth has been debunked through history, and even the government could not provide any data to substantiate its claim. It seems people forgot that slavery of Africans had existed in Canada since the early 1600s, and they were forced to work in deplorable conditions year-round.

---

2 The brief was written to the Prime Minister, the Minister of Citizenship and Immigration, and Members of the Government of Canada and presented to the Minister of Citizenship and Immigration, Walter E. Harris, on Tuesday, April 27, 1954.

3 Ibid.

The pressure placed on the Government by the delegation that went to Ottawa and the constant protests of the Black population, primarily in Quebec and Ontario, were successful in effecting change to the legislation, which in 1962 saw the removal of overt racial discrimination from Canadian immigration policy.

It must be noted, though, that people from the Caribbean began settling in Canada since the late 18th Century. Historic records state that in 1796 a group of between 500 and 600 Maroons (runaway slaves) from Jamaica arrived in Halifax, Nova Scotia[4]. This was a solution employed by the British colonizers to quell the constant uprising of these men and women who refused to be enslaved.

The Canadian Encyclopedia states that between 1800 and 1920, a small group of Jamaicans and Barbadians immigrated as labourers to work in the Cape Breton and Sydney mines. Another wave of immigrants from the Caribbean came after World War II; however, it wasn't until the 1960s and 1970s that large increases in immigration from the Caribbean really began.

Prior to the changes to the Immigration Act of 1962, the Canadian government, along with the British government and its West Indian colonies, established the West Indian Domestic Scheme through which women from the Caribbean were able to immigrate to Canada as domestics

---

4 Source: Caribbean Canadians, The Canadian Encyclopedia. https://www.thecanadianencyclopedia.ca/en/article/caribbean-canadians

and nurses. These women could, after one year of service, pursue other careers, continue their studies, and become residents. They were also allowed to send for their fiancés and family members.

To be eligible for this program, an applicant had to be single with no children, between the ages of 18 and 35 years, have at least a grade 8 education, be medically fit, and pass an interview with Canadian immigration.

In order to be selected, some women who had children did not divulge this fact to the authorities as they wanted the opportunity to travel and/or obtain a better life for themselves and their families. This situation created some complex social dilemmas as the re-unification of these families years later did not always go well.

The labour departments in the West Indian countries encouraged the best and brightest women to apply. Therefore, it was difficult for some of them who had never done domestic work before to adapt to what their new jobs required. Many of these women had trained and worked as secretaries and teachers, and held office jobs. In fact, some of them had come from homes where they had domestic help themselves. However, participating in the scheme was the only way to get to Canada because the immigration laws were so restrictive.

Approximately 3,000 women entered Canada through this scheme, primarily from Jamaica, Barbados, Guyana, Dominica, Trinidad and Tobago, and Grenada. This scheme lasted from 1955 to 1967, when new immigration regulations based on the points system were implemented.

Some of the storytellers in this book came to Canada through the Domestic Scheme and, as you will observe, they have varying tales to tell of their first impressions, experiences, and how they coped with the culture shock of moving to a foreign land.

Immigrating to a new country will always generate some kind of a culture shock, but it is made more difficult if the immigrants do not encounter a welcoming environment in their first few months of settling in. Racism was a major affront to many immigrants. As noted in Frances Henry's article "The West Indian Domestic Scheme in Canada",[5] there were widespread stories of racial discrimination and hostility, some of which are told in this book.

For the first time, many of these new immigrants were made aware of their cultural identity and of their "Blackness" – a concept they hadn't considered before. When coming from a country with a majority or large Black population, one's racial identity is not usually a conscious thought as much as one's social/class status. These new immigrants were, therefore, unprepared for such an awakening.

After fulfilling their one-year duty and wanting to move out on their own, some were refused accommodation due to the colour of their skin or had a difficult time obtaining a

5 This article was originally published by the University College of the West Indies, Institute of Social and Economic Research, in 1968.

job in the field in which they had trained or worked before immigrating to Canada. They did what they had to do to get ahead, and many enrolled in colleges to obtain the relevant qualifications while taking on any type of job to get them through the difficult period.

Not everyone came through the Domestic Scheme. As this program was restricted to women, the men came primarily to study or for short-term vacations and stayed.

Many of the men who came after the war found it extremely difficult, especially in finding employment. One of the only jobs available to them was as a sleeping car porter, a railway employee who attended to passengers aboard sleeping cars. This job demanded long hours for little pay and the Black porters could be fired suddenly for the slightest complaint and were often subjected to racist treatment.[6]

Some immigrants took a circular route, first immigrating to the United Kingdom and then coming to Canada. Their experiences were similar, although coming from the UK, they found racism and prejudice in Canada to be more covert and subtle.

It is important to note that as Canada relaxed its immigration policies in 1962, Britain passed a number of race relations acts making entry for non-white immigrants

---

6 Source: Sleeping Car Porters in Canada, The Canadian Encyclopedia. https://thecanadianencyclopedia.ca/en/search?search=black+porters

more difficult, which resulted in the destruction of the old Commonwealth concept of a family of nations.[7]

The Canadian Immigration Act of 1967 established new standards for evaluating potential immigrants. Regardless of race, ethnicity, or national origin, immigrants received points based on their education, occupation, skills, employment prospects, age, personal character, and proficiency in either English or French. And, in 1971, when the federal government of Prime Minister Pierre Trudeau introduced its multiculturalism policy, it further boosted the opportunity for greater immigration from the Caribbean region.

While entry to Canada was made less difficult, the changes to the immigration policies did not immediately change the systemic racism that is embedded in various institutions or the attitudes of Canadians toward Black people. The fight for equity and equality continues today.

---

7 Flying Fish in the Great White North: The "Culture" of Black Barbadian Migration to 1967 by Christopher S. Taylor. This was his doctoral thesis at the University of Western Ontario.

Donald Moore and the Negro Citizenship Association at a Reception for West Indians in 1954. City of Toronto Archives.

Donald Moore at a tea party held at Donavalon House in 1959. City of Toronto Archives.

DELEGATES TO OTTAWA URGE IMMIGRATION POLICY CHANGE

Ottawa — Spokesmen for the Toronto Negro Citizenship delegation urged Minister of Immigration Walter Harris to lift the color bar in Canada's immigration policy, in a brief presented to the immigration minister last month.

The representation to the Dominion government marked the first time in Canadian history that a Negro organization led a delegation to Ottawa.

The delegation, made up of white and Negro members, was supported by 25 organizations. Among these were:

The Canadian Congress of Labour, The Toronto and Lakeshore Labour Council, United Automobile Workers (CIO-CCL), Locals 439 and 303, Toronto, and Local 222, Oshawa, The United Church of Canada, The Church of England in Canada, The Brotherhood of Sleeping Car Porters, C.P.R. Division, Toronto; The Canadian Negro Women's Club, Toronto; The Home Comfort Club, Toronto; The Negro Citizenship Association, Montreal; The Universal Negro Improvement Association, Montreal; The National Unity Association, Dresden; Chatham and Buxton; The Toronto Negro Veterans Association; and the Canadian Brotherhood of Railway Employees, Local 123.

Don Moore, president of the Negro Citizenship Association, outlined the heroic role that Negroes played in the defense of Canada all down through history and the contribution they made as Canadian citizens.

Addressing the minister of immigration, Mr. Moore asked, "In the light of what you have heard today, in the face of the facts which cannot be denied, in the face of the harm being done to 20,000 Canadians can your department jeoparidize the democratic standards of Canada before the public opinion of the world? Will your department still continue to deny equal treatment to British subjects and citizens of the commonwealth?"

Dr. Norman Grizzle discussed with Mr Harris the ability of people from the tropics to withstand Canadian climatic conditions.

"To date, contrary to some beliefs and utterances," said Dr. Grizzle, "there has been no proof on any basis, scientific, anthropological or otherwise, that the Canadian climate has any adverse affects on persons from tropical areas.

"We conclude on this subject," said Dr. Grizzle, "by saying that the assumption that people from tropical areas are more likely to

(Continued on Page 3)

VOL. 2, NO. 3 TORONTO, APRIL-MAY, 1954 PRICE 10c

Immigration Law Rapped At Citizenship Meeting

Toronto—Charges of discrimination in Canada's immigration policy were heard here last month at a mass meeting held at the Carlton Street United Church by the Negro Citizenship Association.

Don Moore, president of the association, told the gathering of over 200 persons that the immigration restrictions were bringing untold suffering and hardships to people from countries such as the West Indies who try to enter Canada.

Mr. Moore cited the case of a Negro Minister from the West Indies, Rev. Voce, who was detained in the Don Jail when he tried to obtain Canadian Citizenship.

"It took us fifteen months to get a trained nurse from the West Indies into Canada," said Mr. Moore, 'and we only got permission for her to enter after endless letters, wires, cables and phone calls."

Dr. Norman Grizzle, secretary of the organization, gave a detailed report on the immigration policy, showing many instances of how the Immigration Act works to keep dark races out of Canada.

"The immigration department has agencies set up in all countries except those whose people are predominantly Negro or Asian," said Dr. Grizzle, who pointed out that the argument that Negroes do not make good citizens because they cannot assimilate themselves, was wholly unfounded and lacked truth.

"The Ontario Department of Health and Welfare and the University of Toronto have no figures

(Continued on Page 4)

SERIOUSLY ILL

Hamilton—Rev. John Holland who suffered a stroke several weeks ago is still seriously ill in the Hamilton General Hospital. Rev. Holland was chosen "Man of the Year" by the Hamilton Chamber of Commerce recently.

Off for Ottawa

Part of the delegation of the Negro Citizenship Association is shown here boarding the train, at the Union Station, for Ottawa where they presented a brief to Walter E. Harris Minister of Immigration. In the background are (left) Don Moore, president of the Association, and Dr. Norman Grizzle, secretary. In the foreground are Lenore Richardson, corresponding secretary and Val Armstrong, a delegate from the Toronto United Negro Association.

AVRO QUITS GOLF CLUB

Port Credit — The barring of James Marshall, an A. V. Roe employee, from the golf course at the Lakeview Golf Course here, last month caused a storm of public protest and resulted in the

JAMES MARSHALL

cancellation of the Avro Golf tournament which was scheduled to be held at the club May 1.

Mr. Marshall, who won the company's Novice trophy last year, was turned away from the course by assistant greens-keeper Art Taylor.

The refusal was in line with a "standing order from Mr. Purtle," according to greens-keeper James Firth who said the rule had gone into force last year when some club members objected to a Negro playing on the same fairway they were on. Later, however, Mr. Firth said there was no club rule barring Negroes.

When asked if the club had any rule to this effect, the owner of the club, A. W. Purtle, countered with:

"Why pick on us. Why don't you ask some other golf clubs the same question?"

The executive of the 6,000 member local 717, of the international assoication of machinists, (AFL)-(TLC), following a special week-end meeting, sent a letter to the club stating that its members felt the match should not be held on any course that discriminated against Negroes.

NEW FAP ACT EFFECTIVE JUNE 6

The Ontario Legislature recently enacted the Fair Accommodation Practices Act — a law prohibiting denial of "the accommodation, services or facilities available in any place to which the public is customarily admitted" because of race, creed or nationality.

The new act incorporates the provisions of the formal Racial Discrimination Act of 1944, which prohibited publishing or display discriminatory signs — such as "Restricted," "Gentiles Only." It makes illegal the refusal of service or accommodation in any public place—including hotels, resorts, barber shops, beauty parlors and beverage rooms.

Newspaper coverage of the delegation to Ottawa, Apr 27, 1954. City of Toronto.

Our Lives
OUR STORIES

WINSOME BARTON

Keep focused

I was born and raised in Kingston, Jamaica. I had been to the United Kingdom a few times and came to Canada on several occasions to visit my sister and godmother in Montreal. I eventually immigrated to Canada on August 4, 2003, sponsored by my third daughter. She also sponsored her youngest sister, who eventually studied at and graduated from York University with honours.

Initially, I considered Montreal my home, having been there many times. So I moved from Toronto, leaving my daughters and reuniting with my sister. However, I returned to Toronto after a while.

My work experiences have been quite exciting. I was engaged in various types of assignments, including using a cash register, sorting, packaging, etc. I must admit that visiting a country is very different from living in it. In England, I witnessed some white kids in a cricket park telling a Black child, "No Blacks here." I was appalled and upset that such foul words came out of kids. What I experienced in Canada was different. It was more of a jealously from white people. I recall when I had a job in the factory and a white girl wanted my position because she believed what I was doing was easier than the task she had been given. But the truth of it was that I had gained technical proficiency over time from repetition and work experience.

Many a time, people link racism as an issue between Black and white folks. The racism I was exposed to was initially from Indians (South Asians). The warehouse had quite a few South Asians and they would usually show Blacks that they were not welcome. They were in key positions like team lead or supervisor. But it did not matter what they showed me. I do not look for trouble, and I also do not turn around when someone brings it on.

My children had their share of experiences too. But I trained them to always remain focused on their studies, which paid off eventually. What I would say is that the benefit of residing here outweighs the aspects of segregation and discrimination. As a matter of fact, I like to think that my daughter took me out of bondage by sponsoring me to live here, because at that period, I was going through some domestic issues.

In comparison to Canada, Jamaica had some prospects and good jobs, but you had to be very qualified and connected to earn yourself one. There is discrimination there as well. For instance, I knew a lady who studied engineering but ended up as a teacher because she was seen as going into a male-dominated profession.

In summary, everything concerning my immigration has worked for my good and that of my family. My children are settled as well. I have no regrets whatsoever because I can go home to visit Jamaica whenever I want. I will continue to maintain full ties with my country of origin because my parents, who are long gone, are buried there.

CLARICE BAZYONO

Vindicated

Clarice was born in Jamaica. In 1972, she came to Canada to visit her sister, leaving the rest of her family back home. Like many other visitors who came to Canada, at the back of her mind she had come to seek better opportunities in a foreign land.

At that time visitors were not allowed to work without legal documentation, and so Clarice, like many others, worked and received cash below the minimum wage. As a result of such circumstances, she experienced untold hardship for many years. In an effort to look after herself and her family in Jamaica, Clarice worked "around the clock", doing two jobs as a nursing aid.

Clarice is a Christian and a firm believer that every situation she undergoes is bound to end positively. This indeed was confirmed as the Ontario government "miraculously" granted amnesty to law-abiding illegal immigrants. Clarice remembers that period as one of the most challenging to her faith.

The government wanted those who were illegal to appear before an immigration panel. She recalls many failed to show up for fear of deportation. After attending the hearing, Clarice was anxious as she waited for the decision. While she was getting ready to go to work one morning, a lady from the postal service called to inform her that there was a telegram for her. Her fear heightened, and so Clarice asked the lady to read the content over the phone. It was the most exciting news for her: She had been granted amnesty and become landed in her dream country.

After receiving her papers, Clarice decided to further her education. She worked in the day and went to school at night. Upon graduation, her status changed from nursing aid to personal support worker.

One of the first things Clarice did was to sponsor her family to come to Canada. She recalls an incident in Toronto when she went to see the lawyer who was processing her children's immigration documents. When the lawyer finished evaluating her assets, she was informed of her eligibility to sponsor her children.

Clarice worked close to the Queen Street bus terminal, which was the final destination on that route, and so she was usually the first to get on the bus on her way home.

When she boarded the bus on that fateful day, she was still overwhelmed with joy, knowing her children would soon become landed immigrants. Clarice began singing Christian songs. A little later at another stop, she noticed a white woman who looked a little troubled getting on the bus. However, she kept rejoicing and did not pay any attention to her. The lady disembarked soon after, unnoticed by Clarice.

Further down the road, the bus stopped, and the same lady and two police officers rushed into the bus. The woman pointed at Clarice and exclaimed, "That one!" One of the officers immediately asked Clarice to get off the bus. In her confused state, Clarice thought the officer was addressing someone else. The officer insisted that she disembark from the bus immediately, stating that she and another man had robbed the lady of her purse.

Clarice was dismayed and felt her dignity being stripped in a matter of seconds. The first thought that ran through her mind was: *This is a dream*. The reality of the accusation started to sink in as her eyes met the displeasure on the familiar faces of the people who rode with her daily on the same bus.

Both police officers eventually got Clarice off the bus for questioning. One officer was white and the other Black. She recounts the former was quite calm, while the latter was extremely arrogant. The situation evoked instant anger when Clarice could not find any comfort with the aggressive officer, who was the same colour as her. And so she immediately turned on the woman who had accused her falsely and almost choked her. She was apprehended and forced into the troopers' vehicle for questioning. The matter was charged, but the court eventually found Clarice innocent. In fact, she was not the first victim of the accuser.

Although the accusation against her was dismissed, Clarice was traumatized for a very long time. She experienced a severe nervous breakdown and would not go on the same bus she had taken to work for several years. She could not face the passengers who had witnessed the incident. As a result, she took a bus that was an hour earlier to go to work and returned an hour later, after everyone was gone.

Clarice's Christian faith became deeper over the years as she put the bitter past behind. Now in her 70s, she is still doing what she loves to do – offering assistance to those in need, on a smaller scale.

STELLA BENJAMIN

Gained strength from bad experiences

I was born in Guyana and lived a good part of my life there before coming to Canada. My older sister was here first. She had come to Canada in the 1970s and thought it would be beneficial for the rest of her family to join her.

In 1984, my older sister sent for my sister and me to visit her. I did not plan to stay at first because I was only here for the holidays. As a matter of fact, I was married with children at that time. When I got here, my sister asked me if I wanted to go to school, which would mean me staying. I responded negatively because of my husband and kids in Guyana. I eventually figured that she was lonely and needed her family around.

For some reason, my sister kept bugging me to stay, and so I insisted that she speak to my husband. Instead she ignored me and took me to immigration. We eventually got a lawyer. The first time we met the lawyer he asked me why

I wanted to come to Canada. My sister replied saying, "This is my sister, and I need company. I don't have anyone down here with me."

At that time, Canada used to encourage immigration for people to have their families around. If you had immediate family back home, you could sponsor them, which is how my family came.

After the lawyer prepared the paperwork, he referred us to the immigration department at Dundas Street and University Avenue in Toronto. We went upstairs to the counter and handed the worker the slip that the lawyer had given us. My sister told the guy at the counter that I needed to go to school. The gentleman stamped the document without paying any attention. My sister asked if I could work, and he said, "Work? Okay!" Then he put another stamp on the sheet.

I would be able to go to school and work. The man sent us to another woman who would orient me as a newcomer to Canada. When I met with her, she spoke to me about a lot of rules and regulations. I did not like her trying to teach me how I had to eat, bathe, and a bunch of other things I considered nonsense, but I had to go with the flow.

I started school at Bathurst High School. I went there for an upgrade. I really didn't need it; I was one of the brightest in the class, but I had to go through the process.

I received a work permit, and my first job was at a factory making television sets. Back then, it was those big, heavy TVs. I used to assemble some parts for the TV and had to make 350 of them in the morning and another 350 in the afternoon.

I remember I was paid $2.25 an hour. I received a bonus during Christmastime, and it was a five-cent-per-hour raise. The female supervisor would ask me to run errands for her such as buying coffee. One day, I got the wrong coffee, and she threw the coffee on the ground and crushed the cup. Another time, she said to me, “Do you know how you got that colour?” I asked her how, and she said, “You were over-baked, like God put you in the oven, and he forgot about you.”

Right away, something came in my head. I asked her, “Do you know how you got that colour?” I continued, “You didn’t cook.” For two weeks, I was a target because of that comment. What she said was discriminatory and derogatory.

Anyway, my husband’s cousin called me and told me there was a position at his place of work, so I switched jobs. Those days you could just go to the job and start right away. You did not have to go through all this process they go through now like signing papers.

They paid you every two weeks. I liked the job, but I didn’t like the people. The company made parts for airplanes. I had to work on machines that made the wings. The machines were set up to spin the parts, and the parts would come out with raw, sharp edges. There was a tool that smoothed out the wings.

That company used to pay $7.00 an hour. I felt like a millionaire. I was able to send money home. Some of my co-workers would be like, "Stella did you come here in a boat? Did you wear grass skirts?" I let them have the freedom to say whatever they wanted because I needed to stay at the job.

One day, a guy in there called me the "N word", and I told the boss. So he calls the guy over and told him what I reported. He said, "No! Why would I call her a N----?" I insisted that he had and started crying because it seemed like they were on his side and not mine just because he said he didn't do it.

My husband always wanted me to finish up my education, so I went to college to study social work. That was the best decision I ever made. It was rough, but I am glad I had good spousal support. Sometimes when I did not feel like going to school, he would come down, warm up the car, and bring my schoolbooks.

I never regretted immigrating to Canada, even though there were so many bad experiences. All of those things made me stronger and who I am today.

MAVIS BOBB

She is like the Shunammite woman

Her daughter likens her to the Shunammite woman,[8] and anyone who is versed in the Biblical scriptures of 2 Kings, chapter 4, would readily agree that Mavis Bobb epitomises the virtues of this woman.

Her daughter wrote in a college paper that: "Looking at the way my mum lives her life today, and even at the way she lived it when we were growing up, it is a definite pattern to that of the Shunammite woman. She may not have had the wealth, good fortunes, and resources of the Shunammite, but she always strived to be hospitable; not only to those whose path crossed hers, but also to those whose path she set out to cross. It was as if she went out seeking to save those who were lost."

8 A notable woman found in 2 Kings, chapter 4, who took care of the needs of the prophet Elisha.

Born in Guyana (then British Guiana) on October 9, 1927, Mother Bobb or Sister Bobb, as Mavis is affectionately known, followed in her mother's and grandmother's footsteps and has passed that legacy on to her children. It's the legacy of "giving 'til it hurts".

Whether she is in Guyana or in Canada, Mother Bobb's door is always open to anyone who needs help in any way. It could be for a meal, a serious issue, or a talk.

Mavis first came to Canada in the late 1970s to bring up one of her grandchildren. Two of her daughters were living here then. At that time, she spent two years in Canada and formed some lasting friendships. So when she eventually immigrated here in 1994, she easily re-connected with her friends.

She is a devout Christian with a strong faith in God and Jesus. She often repeats Biblical scriptures and approaches everything as if directed by God. You will often hear her say, "Whatever the Lord lays on your heart, do it." She lives with that maxim every day.

Growing up, she was very involved in the St. Luke's Presbyterian Church where she worshipped. In church "productions" (plays), Mavis often held the lead roles especially at Christmas. Mavis sang with the carollers along with her mother who was the lead singer. In addition, she was active in Girl Guides, and she participated in athletics. She enjoyed track and field, especially running the 100, 200, and 4 x 100 relay, and proudly notes she ran the anchor leg in relays.

Mavis learned arts and craft at the Fredericks School of Home Economics in Guyana, which was opened in 1936. On leaving school, she taught for a short period in the home economics department at a local school. After she started having children, she became a full-time housewife. However, that didn't mean she stopped working and earning an income.

The mother of 12 children (two of whom have died), Mavis became an entrepreneur, working from home to create lovely works of art such as raffia slippers, embroidered pillow cases, knitted items, and dainty filet-lace crafts made from flour bags. Her main source of income though, was baking – buns, corn bread, pone, cakes, and salara (a type of turnover) – which she sold to help pay school fees for the children.

Back in those days, you would find Mavis at school fairs, sports tournaments and community events selling her goods. She also sold fish. She would go to the wharf to purchase the fish, and the children would then deliver the fish to the clients.

It was like a revolving door at the Bobbs' home; the house was always filled with people coming in or going out – not just family, but everyone in the neighbourhood. Mavis recalls a time when her youngest son brought home a friend who wasn't feeling well, and she took him to the dispensary (pharmacy). She was asked if the boy was her son, and she said, "Everyone is my own."

Her daughters laughingly said they thought she went overboard with her giving, recounting how they always had to get new clothes because their mother would give away their clothes if she felt someone needed them more than the children did. Another one of her adages is: "Sow a good seed, reap a good harvest."

In her college report, her daughter wrote: "To my mum, there was always room for all who dropped by or whom she would literally bring in from the road to share meals or to bed down – not just for a night, but for as long as they chose. Many times, we would have a whole family of children sharing our humble abode. In the case of adults, particularly the elderly, they were always welcome, not only to have cooked meals, but to the services of her children to do their groceries, fetch water for them, clean their homes and surroundings, or fetch and carry for them when they were sick."

When Mother Bobb immigrated to Canada in 1994, she carried on the same tradition and continued in her role as a blessing to others. She retired before she came here and didn't need to work, but she continued to keep her doors open, welcoming all who passed by and providing for anyone who was in need.

Mavis hasn't forgotten those back home. She packs barrels with products, sometimes eight barrels at a time, to send back to the neighbourhood where she lived. If she hears of a flood or any disaster, she mobilizes her children to gather sufficient items to send "back home".

Mother Bobb currently resides in Brampton, Ontario with five of her ten children, all of whom are in Canada.

Some of her children preceded her in 1989, but while she and the others were awaiting their immigration papers, her husband and a son died. She attends the Crosspoint Christian Reform Church and is a member of the United Achievers' Community Services seniors' group. Up until her 89th birthday, you would find Mother Bobb participating in the activities, reading poems and the Bible without glasses, and singing in the choir.

"Whatever I do is to the honour and glory of God," she says. "Don't give me the praise; give God the praise."

SHIRLEY BONARDY

Canada will always be my home

I was born and raised in the twin-island sovereign state of Trinidad and Tobago, the land of "steel band and calypso". We are the southernmost nation in the Caribbean. The thought of leaving the beautiful landscapes and beaches of my birthplace came as a result of my brother in-law's career pursuit. In 1967, he gained admission to further his studies to be a certified electrician.

My brother-in-law remained in constant communication with my husband while he was in Canada. I recall him calling one day and asking my husband, "Do you have a desire to travel?" My husband delightfully answered, "Yes", and that was it. My brother-in-law went ahead to process sponsorship for both of us, and a new door opened in our lives.

My husband was the first to arrive in Canada in September 1969. I came two months later in November – at the age of 23. I left three brothers and four sisters in Trinidad. The thought of missing them was scary, but I was anxious to come to Canada because I was not going to be alone.

It was the most beautiful experience for me. There was snow on the ground, and this "new" weather was incredibly fascinating. I was overwhelmed with joy to say the least.

I underestimated the power of winter, though, and went job hunting in my summer shoes in downtown Toronto. I did not know any better. A neighbour had told me how I could travel on the train and, after reading the map at the train station, off I went for the first time alone. Acclimatizing was never an issue. I just loved it and amazingly remained healthy – not even having a cold for three years.

We made friends very quickly when we landed. As a matter of fact, my husband met a Canadian man of Irish descent on the first day at work, who remains our friend until now. You could not find anyone nicer than him. At the time we met him, his daughter was only three months old, and he would bring her over to our place during weekends. From the onset, our friend introduced us as "Aunt Shirley and Uncle Lodrick" to his daughter. That child is now a grown woman, and she never changed the way she addresses us.

We were blessed to have such good people around; so much so that I never experienced the bitterness of racism. All was good considering the fact that we were new and got around with so much ease, as if we had been here a while.

We settled down fast, and I looked for work in a publishing firm until someone introduced me to "Manpower". I eventually worked with them and got posted to various places. I commuted all around on the bus, and with that I became familiarized with various places and different cultures.

My husband on the other hand was much luckier than me in the sense that he never had to deal with transportation issues. His friends and coworkers got him around.

After working as contract staff for some time, I found a permanent placement with a pharmaceutical company in September 1970, and I worked with them for 35 years. I worked from the bottom all the way up – from a packager to a tester, and then I was promoted to records and release, which was my position when I subsequently left. After years of working, I was given a pair of white gloves in recognition of good service. I still have those gloves.

My ex-manager was also a very nice and unbiased lady, who treated everybody equally. She encouraged me to apply for positions within the company and made us all feel like one big family.

I think in life you get treated the same way you treat other people. When you work with people and show respect, they show you respect as well. I have no regrets about coming to Canada, and it will always be my home. In the early days, we had our fun mostly on Saturday evenings or in the summer. We would walk down the streets of downtown Toronto, visiting stores and window-shopping.

My husband eventually retired in 2005. At that time, he expressed his desire to return to Trinidad and Tobago. But I wasn't ready. As a matter of fact, Canada had become home to me from the beginning. After so much pressure, I gave in and was forced into early retirement. A reception was held in my honour, and I recall mentioning to the staff that I was going to live my husband's dream because this wasn't my dream. My dream was to reside in Canada and travel to the Caribbean for visits.

We moved back for a little while after I retired from work, but I could not stay too long for health reasons. For an entire year, I went back and forth. We eventually decided to follow the doctor's advice that I remain in Canada. My husband came to visit periodically.

Then my husband took ill, and so we decided to re-evaluate the situation, taking into consideration the healthcare system in Trinidad and Tobago. It was basically no match to what we experience here. As a result, my husband agreed that we head back to Canada permanently. We sold all we had taken down but left a few things for memories' sake. Three years later, his condition worsened, and he passed on to glory.

I will always say that I love Canada. I have met good and genuine people here. Although things have changed in regards to safety, the memory that sticks in my head is of a people who were trusting. I remember some days we left our doors unlocked and went to work, and everything remained as we left it.

JAMES BROWN

When you fall, pick yourself up and move on

I was born in Jamaica in 1931, and I came to Canada in 1999. To be honest, I did not have the desire to come to live here. I would say it was pretty much by force, through our son's sponsorship, that my wife and I landed here.

I wanted to go back home when I arrived because of the nature of jobs, which I knew nothing about. When you come here, even if you have an education, you have to "box it" and go back to school. I cried when we first came here. I wanted to go back because I felt I was too old to work in factories.

When my son came with Jamaican qualifications, he had to go to George Brown College because each time he went for an interview, over the phone or one-on-one, he was told he was too qualified for the position he applied for or he didn't have the relevant Canadian experience. Apparently it was very difficult securing a job as a new immigrant.

I had to come out of retirement and get a job. I worked at a warehouse. I never knew about warehouses back home. We knew about factories, but not warehouses. My wife did the personal support worker course, because back home she used to work in that field for a while before starting her own business. She had to work at night and did not drive. Therefore, she was sometimes on the street taking the bus at 11 p.m. I worried about her.

I recall a story she told about one day when she was coming from work, wearing a hat, and a heavy wind blew it away. She exclaimed, "God, I don't think I deserve this." Every day, she would say to me that she wanted to go back home.

In the winter, sometimes I fell on the way to work. I would get up and continue the trip, calling my wife at some point to book an appointment for me to see the doctor. Many times we fell while running to catch the bus.

When we came, we were staying with our son. We worked doing odd jobs, saved up money, and rented an apartment. After getting our own place, things began to pick up. We started talking to people and feeling more comfortable and happy. Right now, we are thanking God for the opportunity, but it was rough when we first arrived here.

At the end of the day, we are happy. We thank our son and his wife for sponsoring us.

IRENE CARR

Accept the things you cannot change

My name is Irene Carr. I was born in 1940 and grew up in the town of New Amsterdam, Berbice, Guyana (then British Guiana). On February 19, 1977, my husband and I and our three young children moved to Canada. With the help of family and friends, we quickly settled in the Brampton, Ontario, area.

Since I worked with Royal Bank of Canada in Guyana, it was easy to get back into the banking system. I re-joined the company at its newly relocated head office facilities management department, which had just moved from Quebec to Royal Bank Plaza at Bay and Front Streets in Toronto.

Here is where my challenges began. I had to understand and relate to the dominant presence of prejudice from Quebec against those from the Toronto area. Everyone seemed to be like me though – lost in this new location. But

I quickly got myself integrated into the system, and accepted and tried to understand what was happening.

In the 1980s, one could not help but notice the discrimination on the subway and buses. There were stares and looks of scorn, and the fact that a person would wilfully move away to another seat when you sat down. Of course, this has all changed for the better in the past 40 years. I had to accept those things and now have totally gotten over it.

I attended Ryerson University, where I completed the Institute of Canadian Bankers certificates in technology, administration, and business management, while being involved with the bank's social and volunteer activities. Later I was awarded a Certificate of Distinction from the Royal Bank of Canada Charities Fund and the RBC Special Achievement Award for Teamwork with Facilities Management.

In 1999, I officially retired from head office in Toronto and tried doing what I enjoyed – pie making – but I could not continue without the appropriate physical help. So I went back into being trained by RBC for teller's duties and was employed by them on a contractual basis, working on-call at most of the branches in the Peel Region. I thoroughly enjoyed this activity and officially retired from the work force in 2010.

Throughout my time in Canada, I have always been involved with community activities, especially because of our kids (one boy and twin girls) and their social activities.

Now in their forties, they are still involved with soccer and gymnastics.

There are many programs that have moulded my attitude to life at the present time. I have been involved with United Achievers Club, United Achievers' Community Services Inc., United Achievers Non-Profit Housing (where I received the Volunteer Service Award), Victoria Order of Nurses Volunteer Program, Peel Manor Seniors' Singing Program, Holland Christian Homes Seniors' Singing Program, and many church activities.

All in all, I have no regrets whatsoever about coming to Canada because the privileges my family and I have enjoyed here we could not have experienced in Guyana.

DOROTHY CORNELIUS

Two buses, two trains, and another bus

I wasn't looking to leave Jamaica, but the opportunity fell in my lap. I was a 27-year-old nursing assistant with four kids, when the immigration official came around the hospital with applications asking us: "Does anyone want to travel?"

I wasn't the typical applicant, because to be part of the Domestic Scheme you needed to be single and without children, so I stayed quiet about mine. There were other women who did so as well; you just didn't say anything.

I arrived in May 1968 and, on arrival, I was picked up from the airport and taken to the Ford Hotel along with many other women who came as part of the program. We were then dispatched to different parts of Canada. I was the last one on the list for Ontario.

The family I went to work with lived on Old Yonge Street. The husband was a doctor. They needed me to care for their three children. The job didn't interest me and because I hadn't paid my own fare to come to Canada, I was obliged to stay in domestic work for a prescribed period of time.

I left the family after seven months and took a job in a factory, working the overnight shift. I soon discovered that working nights was not for me. By 2 a.m., my eyes were closing, and I struggled to keep up with the packaging work that came through at a steady pace.

When I was laid off from the factory, I already had another iron in the fire. I had applied for a role at Sunnybrook Hospital and was waiting to hear back. They didn't have anything in nursing but offered me a position in the housekeeping department and I jumped at it.

At the time, I was living in an apartment at Oakwood and Eglinton. Sunnybrook was not close, and I didn't drive. It took me two buses, two trains, and another bus to get to and from work, but I wasn't deterred. Even though I wasn't doing the same work as I did back home, and I had new deductions like union dues and a pension plan that were foreign to me, I was very comfortable at Sunnybrook and ended up staying for 32 years until I retired.

In 1973, my son encouraged me to get my drivers' license. I hadn't thought about it before, but it seemed like a good idea. My first good car was a two-toned Chevy station wagon with the wood panels on the side. I paid $900 for that car, and I remember driving around and feeling so proud.

The car changed our lives in other ways and not just for my kids. I would take everyone's kids to school, and we would pile in to go swimming and here and there. Having a car made us mobile and allowed us to more easily access things outside our neighbourhood, which made a huge difference.

Being a single mom raising four kids wasn't easy, and it meant that from an early age my kids needed to be independent, responsible, and resourceful. One day I came home from work to find a burnt-out pot on the ground at the front door. When I asked for the story, my 10-year-old told me that she was making french fries for her siblings – who were 8, 6 and 4 at the time, when the oil caught on fire, and she had to call the fire department.

Luckily no one was hurt. It was equally lucky that the fire department didn't report the incident to the local authorities.

Being a Black woman in Canada in the late 1960s and 1970s wasn't always easy. A number of the women who came to Canada at that time ended up going back to Jamaica because they had good jobs at the post office or in a company at home, and when they came to Canada, they weren't respected in the same way.

There was racism. You would feel it when you went into stores. People would walk away or not offer to help you. They would just pretend that we weren't there.

One time I was on Bloor Street, and I was looking at this nice black coat with fur on the sleeves and collar; it was fancy.

The saleswoman came up and offered her opinion saying, "I don't think that will suit you." She then picked up a big, wide Italian plaid – it was the ugliest coat in the store – and offered it to me. I had a couple of experiences like that, but I knew why I was here and I knew that I belonged.

I am Canadian. I feel Canadian. I built my life here.

LORNA CUSHNIE

I did what I had to do

I might not have come to Canada if it weren't for my husband, David. He had just finished a welding certificate in the United Kingdom, and friends in Canada wrote to tell him about the opportunities for jobs in the Canadian construction industry.

I was comfortable in Britain, having settled there from my West Indian homeland, Nevis. I was a state-registered nurse and state-certified midwife with a six-month old daughter. For sure we had experienced racism, but it was very open and not subtle at all. One landlord told us outright, "We don't let to Blacks." That kind of behaviour was common.

On January 23, 1965, our ship, the SS *Carinthia*, docked at Port 21 in Halifax, Nova Scotia, and the three of us disembarked. It had been a rough sailing, and we arrived one day late due to a storm at sea. It was especially rough for me because I was newly pregnant with our second child. We were officially landed immigrants as we were recruited by Canadian immigration in London, England.

Our final destination was to be Hamilton, Ontario, where I had secured a job at Henderson General Hospital on Hamilton Mountain. For almost three weeks, we looked unsuccessfully for housing and childcare. When I found a daycare, they told me that my daughter was too young. When we found an apartment, they told us it was already rented.

I ended up having to turn down the job and we moved to Montreal where we had friends who could help with childcare. In Montreal, we found a studio apartment within walking distance of the hospital where I had found a job. Childcare was tricky because I needed someone who could care for my daughter when I worked different shifts, including overnight.

From February to May, I worked at the hospital and saved as much as I could. David travelled back to Toronto to look for work and ended up finding a job that paid $1.25 per hour.

At that time, you couldn't work beyond seven months gestation, so when I finished working at the end of May, I moved from Montreal to Toronto to join David.

For the first two years, I didn't feel settled in Canada, and I wasn't sure I was going to stay. Despite being state-certified in Britain, the College of Nurses of Ontario determined that I was 10 hours short of the classroom requirements for a Canadian nurse, so I had to take a qualification exam before I was able to be a registered nurse.

Obviously, I did settle into life in Canada. I got a job in labour and delivery, which was similar to midwifery, so I was doing the kind of work that I was trained to do.

It was a difficult marriage, and I've joked before that the best things that came out of my marriage was the decision to come to Canada, my three kids, a lifelong friendship with a woman who cared for my kids like they were her own, and a cat named Prince Charming (we called him Prince), who I loved dearly.

By 1972, I was a single mother raising three kids on my own. Professionally, I had moved into psychiatric nursing at the Queen Street Mental Health Centre and found a new passion for mental health and well-being, and for leading teams.

Three weekends each month, I worked at The Wellesley Hospital, first as casual staff then as part of the regular weekend team. One weekend per month, I was home with the kids and we'd do something special, including dressing up and going to church.

My kids learned a lot of responsibility. They had weekly rotations for the housework, taking turns cooking, washing dishes, or vacuuming. From tallest to smallest, everyone had a job.

I'm proud of my accomplishments at work. By the time I retired from Queen Street Mental Health Centre in 1998, I was a nurse manager with 31 years of service and a lifetime of experiences that I would never trade.

The hard work came at a cost. I had no social life. I worked and I came home, but I'm not bitter about it. I knew I had to take care of my kids, and I knew that Canada was the best place to do that. I did what I had to do. I worked Sundays, and I worked holidays. I set that example for my kids. We still laugh that at different times all of my kids have had full- and part-time jobs at the same time, because that is what they grew up seeing; that was their normal.

In 1998, the same year I retired, I graduated from York University with a Bachelor of Arts in Sociology. It took me 16 years to finish my degree, taking one class per year. Walking across the stage in front of my children and four grandchildren to receive my degree was another proud moment born of hard work.

If I were giving advice to new Canadians or to myself when I was a new Canadian, I would tell them not to dwell in the past. Focus on your goals for a better life and remember to be thankful for where you are while you build the future you want.

LEE FRANCIS

Facing the highs and lows

Lee Francis was a carefree young man, and therefore it was not surprising when in May 1955, he left the shores of his homeland, Jamaica, to join his sister and brother in England.

Lee's sister and brother were a part of the trend of Jamaicans who were moving to England at that time. He heard of the many opportunities in England and was challenged by the lack of opportunities in Jamaica, so he decided to make the move.

The journey was a very exciting time for him. He travelled on a ship, which stopped in Italy, Spain, Switzerland, and France along the way to his destination. He recalls visiting a bull ring in Barcelona, Spain, but didn't have an opportunity to see the bulls fight, as they weren't scheduled to do so until later that day.

In those days, it was challenging for Black people in England. Finding lodging was hard because there were limited places to rent due to the fact that many areas were still war-torn, and many places would not rent to Black people. Some even displayed signs that boldly said, "No Blacks". Many Black people had to resort to renting a bed and sharing a room with three or four strangers.

He remembers that the way some people managed to afford housing was through their participation in a "partner", whereby they would buy a house with the proceeds and rent it out to their friends. (A "partner" is a form of co-operative in which people save collectively. There is one person who collects the funds and distributes the pool of money on a rotating basis to the various participants.) Fortunately for Lee, he was able to take his brother's old rental place when his brother found somewhere else to live.

The first job that Lee got in England was to move around steel rods. He was fortunate to work with two other Jamaicans, so it was a bit like home. But the pay wasn't good and he decided to move on. He found a plumbing union and secured a job in his area of expertise. He made twice the amount of money and stayed in that position for nine months. After that, he moved on to another company where he worked for 11 years. He had the opportunity to work on site at the Bank of England.

"You would just do your work and go home. No one bothered you. There wasn't any security or cameras," states Lee. While working in London, he recalls seeing famous

Russian politicians Nikita Khrushchev and Nikolai Bulganin in person at Grosvenor Square.

In the fall of 1966, Lee decided to leave England because it was too crowded there with people and traffic. His sister had immigrated to Canada, so he decided to move here as well. He journeyed by ship, which docked in Quebec City, and took a train to Toronto. He found a place to live but it was horrible, so he only stayed there for a month. Within a few months of arriving in Canada, he bought a house with money he had saved in England.

Lee started looking for work, but soon realized that a license was required to do plumbing work in Canada, so he applied for one. He found work, but didn't find a steady job for a long time. He had to do what he had to do. He even worked for a very low hourly wage. He went wherever he could to find work ranging from Sarnia to Western Canada.

Life was challenging, the wages were low, and it was very cold. "If I didn't have family here, I probably would have gone back to England back then," he says. He faced some racism in Canada as well. He would work jobs on pipes in the dirt, and as soon as the job site was clean, he would get laid off.

However, the situation improved over the years. Lee has been a member of plumbers' union Local 46 for 53 years, and he still actively participates by helping recent grads find opportunities.

Despite the harsh beginning, Lee believes he made the right decision to move to Canada. The 1980s and 1990s were particularly difficult because of the boom and bust economy, when stocks went down, investment values plummeted, and many people lost their jobs. Conversely, he remembers the days when gas was $0.28 a gallon, and cars and homes were cheap. He faced some highs and lows, but Canada is his home.

LYNN FRANCOIS

Strong family bonds

In 1962, the Government of Canada tabled legislation eliminating overt racial discrimination in its immigration policy. Prospective immigrants could no longer be denied entry to Canada on the basis of colour, race, or nationality. This change, combined with a *1966 White Paper on Immigration*[9] that recognized immigration as a major contributor to the population and economic growth, were part of the tailwinds that brought me and 15 other Dominican women together at the Ford Hotel in downtown Toronto in 1968.

When the opportunity to come to Canada came up, I jumped on it. I was in school studying nursing, but I wanted to see what the world looked like. My older brother was

9 White Paper on Immigration, 1966, Retrieved from the Canadian Museum of Immigration at Pier 21: https://pier21.ca/research/immigration-history/white-paper-on-immigration-1966

away, and my older sister was in St. Croix, so it was my turn to travel.

Despite never having worked as a domestic at home, I was accepted as part of the West Indian Domestic Scheme. The 15 women and I arrived during the Victoria Day weekend and, by Monday, each of us was sent off to live with our employer family. My employer lived in Forest Hill. They had three children and my role was to take care of the children.

After the initial one-year commitment, I ended up staying with the family for another five years while I attended school at George Brown College and took business courses. From there, I worked at George Brown and held a number of other jobs until I retired 37 years later. Over the years, I was employed in payroll and accounting working with international students, at Jobs Ontario working with students and employers, and finally in investment banking. It was nothing that I could have imagined doing when I was a child, but I loved doing it.

When I came to Canada, there were so many of us, we were able to stick together. Often there were parties and all of us would attend. We would stay overnight and then wake up and make breakfast together.

In Dominica, we didn't know prejudice. The only time that racism hit me in the face was one time on a TTC bus. My sister Clem and I were travelling on the bus, and there was an old white man sitting there. For some reason, Clem moved and when she did, the old man moved up as well.

Clem looked at me, and I looked at her, and we thought, *Let's have some fun.* She moved up again, and he stood up. When he did that, the bus driver looked at him and shook his head; he understood what was happening. When the old man left the bus, the driver shrugged and said to us, "People don't change," and that was it. With racism, you just have to say, "That is their problem, not mine."

I live in Canada, but I'm still Dominican. Our house is still there, and I could go back and live for a few months at a time. If I had stayed in Dominica, my life would have been different. I wouldn't have gotten married when I wanted to get married because my parents would have told me when to marry and whom I should marry. And I would probably have ended up having three or four kids. I would probably still be there.

Instead of looking back, I look forward. I love to travel and to stay in touch with family and friends; keeping those bonds strong is important to me. I am still in contact with some of the women with whom I went to school. One of them lives in Corpus Christi, and we travel together. Another classmate is in Texas. Strong family bonds don't have to change with time or distance; it just takes a little more effort.

VICTORIA FRASER

Believe in someone

I learned about Canada from the guest lecturers who taught at our teacher's college in Trinidad. Through their descriptions, many of us became interested and enthused about the country.

My first chance to come to Canada came in 1971, when I moved with our two little ones in tow to Edmonton and joined my husband who was already there studying and working.

We lived and worked close to the university, where it was more common to see people from all over the world. Yet I still had occasion to meet and work with people who had not seen any West Indians before meeting me.

There was even an incident when I worked in the kitchen of the Faculty Club, and I got cut with a glass. Somebody who came to Canada from Ireland really wanted to see what my blood looked like because she couldn't believe that it would be red too. So that was a bit of amusement. We had studied Canada in our nature studies, and we didn't think that Canadians lived in igloos, but I guess not everyone had that background.

They didn't know where we were or what sort of lives we lived before coming here. But at the same time, I had very good relationships, and people were generally warm and welcoming. There was a lot of curiosity and many things they didn't know, so when a question was asked, I answered it. I took it in stride because I knew I was imparting new knowledge.

In these times, I feel something a little different. There seems to be fear, and that's the part that I don't enjoy. The way some people react to Black people, and in particular Black youth, is to gather up their children and their belongings as if they are scared. I see it in my volunteer work as well. When someone comes in looking for help, they don't ask me first, or if they do and someone else appears, they are immediately done with me and they go for the same advice and the same answer from another person.

Between 1971 and 2002, I moved back and forth, living and working in both Canada and Trinidad, including educational exchanges and school visits.

On one visit, I was sitting in the office waiting for the principal, and there was a half wall so you could just see my hair as I was sitting there. A young man was called to the office to be my guide for the day. When he rounded the corner and we came face-to-face, he exhaled, slumped a little, and said,

"I thought it was my mother. I thought I was in trouble." And I realized that was something that could happen to any Black child here. They get in trouble and don't really even know why. They tend to be the focus of attention when things go bad. When there is something good, they aren't necessarily the ones that are chosen.

In that moment, I said to myself that if any other Black child should see me, I want them to see me in a positive situation. That encouraged my involvement in volunteering.

After my retirement, I came back to Canada to live and raise my grandchildren. I jumped in with both feet and started volunteering – first at church and then at the children's school. I was involved with re-stocking books in the library, attending field trips if they were a teacher short, planting a garden, leading the choir, and planning Black History Month celebrations. I also had the opportunity to bring a part of the Caribbean into this community by starting a steel band club at the school.

At the end of one term, another parent and I hosted a West Indian lunch. We prepared our favourites including mauby, sorrel, sweet bread and red fish, and all was well received. Things are probably different now because of allergies and food sensitivities, but at the time, it was great to celebrate together and create this different experience for these groups of children.

Currently, I volunteer with Toastmasters. I see some kids who need a lot of encouragement, and I try to be there for them. If you get involved, you can make a difference.

My mother never indulged in the politics of differences. We had relatives from all over the West Indies, so I didn't ever see "small island" differences. I can interact with people from many places, especially India, because in Trinidad we have five main cultures, and Indian is one of them. We grew up with all people, and I enjoyed some aspects of other cultures.

I really keep it foremost that I want to encourage these children here. I don't mind being involved to show the kids that we need to be involved. I need to be involved so that they see me as being part of the establishment, and they realize that they can be as well.

Even though I'm getting older, it's getting colder, and it's a long bus ride, I decided to renew my membership in the Toastmasters group to have a louder voice in the decision-making process and a greater impact.

Our children need to see examples of us being out there participating in the community and for them to understand that they need to get out there too.

RITA GAYLE

I AM the guy

I was 21 years old when I arrived in Canada on September 20, 1968. I'm from a large family. My mother had nine kids, and we struggled after my father walked out. We had nothing. My big sister, Janet, started working at 16 years old. She was very bright, and she worked hard and sacrificed to make sure that all of us had a good education.

After school, I got jobs here and there, but I wasn't pleased about my career. In Jamaica, the fair-skinned people were the ones who got the jobs whether they were educated or not. We had that prejudice. I decided to better myself, and that's when I decided that I wanted to go abroad.

I was hoping it would not be the United States because I wasn't very fond of the US, and then I learned about Canada. I told a friend about my application, and she quickly dismissed it, saying, "You'll never get to go to Canada. Canada only takes white people...so you'll never go to Canada."

Once my application was accepted, I never looked back. I came alone with US$500 and knowing only one other person in Canada. Within two weeks of landing at Lester B. Pearson Airport, I had rented a room and accepted my first Canadian job.

When you are alone, you have strength because you know you have to sink or swim. I learned to swim really fast because there was no one to rely on. I got lost on the subway so many times, but that taught me where to go. Even though I had never seen a subway before coming to Canada, I learned to navigate and to get around.

I worked at North American Life Insurance Company processing death claims for two years before moving to United Artists to work for an advertising manager. Following a promotion as the assistant to the general manager, I was in charge of screening new movies. When a new movie was about to be released, I would go to a theatre to watch the movie alongside the reporters and movie critics.

One time, I attended a screening but something happened, and they were late to start the film. I went to the projectionist and asked why we were waiting, and he told me that he was waiting for "the guy" to get here. I smiled and told him, "I am the guy." He didn't believe a woman could have that position much less a Black woman. He looked me up and down, sensed my resolve, and started the movie.

My husband was studying air conditioning, so we moved to Chicago and lived there for four years. After he graduated, we came back to Canada, and I couldn't wait. Now that I had a comparison, I knew that I really liked it here.

While we were in the US, we saved all our money so that we could buy a house. When we came back to Canada, we moved to Brampton and bought a semi-detached house off Linkdale Road in 1976. We accomplished our goal!

I opened my first bank account with CIBC bank in 1968. Ten years later, I joined the bank; first as a secretary, then as a loans officer and financial advisor. Over my 30 years at the bank, I received peer and customer accolades and built a lifetime of memories.

When I first came to Canada, I really felt like I wanted to go home because I felt so lonely. I couldn't believe that there were so few Black people. But when I got to know the people I worked with, then I felt more at home.

Thirty years ago, I sponsored my big sister Janet to come to Canada. She is the only one of my siblings who is here. She really loves Canada, and I love having her around.

ELMA HAMILTON

If at first you don't succeed, keep on trying.

In 1967, at 28 years of age, I came to Canada as a landed immigrant with the intention of getting a job. In Trinidad, I was working at a Credit Union doing secretarial work, and I assumed that I could get a similar job here in Canada.

Right away, I started looking, phoning and applying for a job. I would send my resume in advance and secure an interview, but when I arrived, and they looked at me, the story changed, and suddenly I needed "Canadian experience".

For one opportunity, my interview was supposed to be at 10 a.m. and at 11:30 a.m., I was still there and had not been seen by anyone. Other people came, were interviewed, and left, but I was still waiting. One woman said that they should be calling me soon, but that "soon" never came because they came out and said that the person who was supposed to interview me was going on lunch.

I had something to eat and when I came back, there was no sign of my application. It was gone. It was like I didn't exist.

It was frustrating, but I realized that I had to change my mindset. Instead of looking for the job that I felt I would be comfortable in, I had to get a job – any job. I kept reading the papers and applying for positions. I memorized my Social Insurance Number because I used it so often on applications.

I finally secured a job working in the scheduling department of Toronto East General Hospital. It paid $3.10 per hour and took me six months to land, but I was excited to have it. I worked at the hospital for nine months, and all the while, I continued to look for my next opportunity, my next role.

Being disrespected didn't only happen in the work environment. One time, when I was walking home, a car drove up beside me. The driver asked if I wanted a ride home, and naturally I declined. He called out again, and when I looked down, I noticed that he was exposing himself.

At those times, when they saw Black women, they thought that we were just out for fun. When you went to the theatre downtown to watch a movie, you had to be careful not to leave an empty seat beside you because someone might sit down and start fondling you. I experienced that.

I ended up getting a job with the Federal Government, assigning newly created postal codes to addresses all across Canada. Each day, we were given the book of postal codes and a list of addresses. The work was to look up the address to determine its postal code. Each day, we were expected to work through 500 addresses. I took the job, but I never stopped looking for another. I stayed with the Federal Government, but I quickly moved on from that department. I still had to apply for roles, but the discrimination that I faced when I was new to the country was a thing of the past.

Because of the difficultly I had in finding a job, I didn't encourage my family to come to Canada. I sponsored one nephew to come here, but the rest of my family was well established at home and had no need to travel.

Now, I enjoy being a dual citizen of Canada and Trinidad and Tobago and proudly hold two passports. I wasn't a young woman when I left Trinidad, but I certainly did a lot of growing up in Canada.

MICHAEL HAREWOOD

God never left his side

Barbados was where Michael (Mike) Harewood was born and raised. It's a small island – 166 square miles or 431 km^2 – with limited natural resources and thus offered limited options. Therefore, when the opportunity to move to Canada was presented, Mike jumped at the chance.

At the age of 27, Mike and his wife immigrated to Canada, leaving their children behind, and settled in Scarborough. His sister-in-law, her husband, her mother, and other family were already in Canada.

He had heard that there were many opportunities and that Canada was a promising place. He had never travelled abroad before, and he was excited about seeing snow and experiencing a different way of life.

Mike had held a few jobs after completing school and his last position before leaving the island was that of a customs officer. The way that things traditionally worked in Barbados at that time was that as soon as a young person completed high school, they could get a job, primarily in the government or in administrative work within a company.

When Mike left Barbados in October 1971, the island's main sources of revenue were sugar and tourism, but the island was experiencing some difficult times. The quotas for sugar production were not being met and had to be lowered over time. The youth who pursued post-secondary education went abroad, and they weren't returning to Barbados to cut sugar cane. The potential pool of workers was aging and decreasing in size.

Tourism was taking over as the number one foreign exchange earner, which was not optimal as one hurricane could change that in a moment. At that time, there was a steady outward movement. Many people were leaving Barbados and moving to the United States, Canada, and England.

His first job after arriving in Canada was on the loading dock at a Sears warehouse. It was hard work, especially having to work outside in the cold. After the seasonal peak ended, he was laid off. He went to a government office where they regularly posted jobs, but he didn't see anything. He spoke to one of the employees who said that she thought the city was hiring, so she gave him a piece of paper and told him where to go.

Mike went there and was hired as a garbage man. It paid well, and they had medical benefits. He was fortunate to get into this position as his brothers-in-law had been trying to get in for years without any success as this area of work was dominated by Italians. He had great co-workers who made work as fun as possible. In spite of it all, it was a very cold Canadian winter, and Mike found himself hanging off the side of a garbage truck, picking up garbage. He recalls thinking to himself, "I left home as a customs officer and now I'm out in the cold everyday collecting garbage." He didn't want to do that for another winter.

Mike took courses to upgrade his skills, which were a prerequisite for a machine shop position. He lived in Welland, Ontario, for six months in order to complete the course. It was a very small and close-knit community. Also residing in Welland were Black people who came in from the Caribbean to work in the community as seasonal workers, picking fruit in Niagara. Mike recalls his excitement at seeing the first Black person there. She was a maid who worked for someone in the area.

It was a challenging time. He felt isolated, and the local people weren't friendly. He took the bus home on weekends, but dreaded the long bus ride back on Sundays. Upon completion of the course, Mike got a job at a small machine shop in Richmond Hill. He worked there for two years, but resigned because he wasn't comfortable at his job, and he made less than he did as a garbage man.

He was hired at Canadian Tire, where he worked until his retirement in 1996. It was a good company that paid well and had benefits and profit sharing. He started out in shipping and receiving, was promoted to a shipping and receiving manager, and eventually became a project manager. He was hand-picked by management to travel to the United States to take a methods analyst course. He says this caused some jealousy because some workers wondered why he as a Black man was chosen to go and take that course.

Mike is a firm believer in being fair, equitable and treating people with respect. He had a subordinate that was a good worker, however, this worker did everything he could to undermine Mike because Mike was Black and his superior. It was so blatant that his managers noticed it, and they turned down the employee's annual requests for wage increases.

However, Mike interceded for this individual and asked them to give him a raise because he was a good worker. Sometime later, that employee was a key part of Mike's team who helped to break productivity records. He was later promoted and sought Mike's advice and guidance on preparing his first memo. Mike states: "As Black people in positions of authority, we don't need to tell people that we're up here and they're down there. How one conducts oneself is important, and it teaches one humility. Respect others, and they'll respect you."

For a number of years after retirement, Mike was called in on occasion by a former manager to fill short-term management positions.

One interesting point that Mike mentions is that when he came to Canada, he didn't really go to church much. The North American way of life had many distractions and pressures. Back home, he grew up going to church multiple times a day each Sunday. Therefore, he always had Christian principles in his heart and is thankful that God never left his side.

Mike is now busier than ever. He spends his time between home, church, and volunteering. He is very involved in his local church and volunteers at a local food bank and a retirement home.

In regards to coping with moving to a different country, Mike says he put his priorities in order, and once they were in order, he found that he could cope with most things. There were times when it was better to observe, learn, and keep his mouth shut.

Mike had a happy and safe life in Barbados, and everyone looked out for each other; however, the opportunities just weren't there. Mike knows that moving to Canada was the right choice. He has lived a very good life here and is glad that he came. He learned to appreciate things, broadened his horizons, and met good people who influenced him in many ways. He would not go back to Barbados to live but will visit. His life is here in Canada.

MITZIE HARRIS

Money cannot buy joy

I was born in Jamaica. I grew up and was schooled there as well. Life was family-oriented back home, so when I started looking to travel abroad, most of my people frowned at the idea. But eventually I could not be bothered with their thoughts, and so I opted to make a move and ended up in Canada on September 30, 1973.

At the time, I just wanted to have a different experience of life and cultures. So when the Ministry of Labour sent out invitations to have contractors come into Canada, I applied.

Migrating to Canada was a totally different experience. The culture was different, and the caregiver program was interesting. I was interested to see the comparison between the upbringing of a Canadian child and a Jamaican. That was my main reason for entering under this program.

I was assigned as a live-in caregiver to a family consisting of a single mother and three kids. The experience, however, was not the best. We were well prepared in Jamaica, but the Canadians did not prepare the families well enough to receive us.

That being said, there wasn't much information on Canada as a country. I was aware that it was in North America and that it was a first-world country. However I did not know much about the country's operations. We were uneducated in that department. We had to go and experience living there first. I came alone with no family members, as it was just an adventure, which has lasted 44 years.

They did not have any community groups then, and so we had to get together with one another from the same culture in order to feel a sense of community. We had to adjust to living with Canadians and forget about our own culture. It was very hard to adjust to a different lifestyle. Some Canadians wanted to work things out, but not everyone was on the same page.

One would expect that I would have returned home to Jamaica with such challenges, but I chose to stay and weather the storm. Most people were dying to have the same experience back home, and so it was rare that those who came would want to go back. Those who returned had very rough times or records with the law enforcement agencies. When I came here and got settled, the immigration system was extremely helpful; they even encouraged you to sponsor family members.

I have learned over the years that money cannot buy joy or change our experiences when it comes to dealing with people who are culturally mismatched. I do not have many regrets other than my first job, the effects of which lasted a long time. The family I was assigned to was quite unpleasant, and we did not get along.

After a while of trying to manage things, I got fed up with the family I had offered services to as caregiver. I consulted with the immigration office for advice, and they advised me, "You are now an immigrant. Go out and find a new job."

Overall, I cannot say everything was bad for me as a result of Canadians being unfriendly. I was inexperienced and unexposed to lots of things. As time went by, I matured, learned my way around, and gained sufficient Canadian experience to quit complaining.

I love it here, and I believe with proper orientation any newcomer will enjoy this country.

NESSA HIGHGATE

Judge people by their character

I left my country, Jamaica, for England at a very young age. I was 10 years old to be precise. My grandmother raised me during my tender years, and I owe her so much. My mom, on the other hand, had relocated to the United Kingdom to build her life.

In the Caribbean, it is not unusual for members of extended families like aunts, uncles, and grandparents to raise the kids for their relatives who are unable to do so or who are dysfunctional.

It is funny that I am sharing my story because my seven-year-old grandchild was trying to figure out why I have two names, Nessa and Pam. When I was born in Jamaica, I was called "Nessa", which is my birth name. When I reunited with my mom in England, my mom started calling me "Pam". My guess is it was trendier or more sophisticated to call me that instead of Nessa. But I switched back to being called Nessa as soon as I became independent and comfortable with the colour of my skin. However, I kept both names.

A while ago, when a young family member of mine got pregnant, she said, "I'm thinking of sending the baby home to my mother until she is of age." I advised her not to send the baby home. I thought it was better she have the baby with her to help them bond. I never bonded with my mother; I bonded with those who were there for me in my early life, like my aunt and my grandmother. I never addressed my mother as "mom" until I lived with her.

My mom and my stepfather left England when I was 16 years old. As a matter of fact, it was obvious the economy was bad, and Canada had opened up immigration. And so we left England and came here. I was reluctant to undertake the journey. I was 16, I had made some friends, and I was planning to go into nursing. I wanted to remain in England. If I were older, I would have had my way.

Surprisingly, I adjusted quickly when I arrived in Canada. I went straight to high school, and after that, I went into a hospital to train as a nurse. In those days, all nursing training was done in the hospitals. The colleges took it on much later, and today the universities are offering nursing programs.

I was successful in the program and became a nurse at the age of 21. I have been a nurse my entire life. It was my passion, and I never regretted being a nurse.

One of the biggest things that helped with my transition into Canada was that the British system had similarities. Also, I became proficient with the English language, of which I articulated well.

In terms of the weather, I actually preferred Canadian weather. I honestly believed then that it was better to have the various seasons than the constantly damp British weather. Secondly, Canadians prepared better in the winter with appropriate clothing and central heating systems in their homes.

Jamaicans are naturally proud and ambitious, and so others find it difficult to understand our culture. We were not exposed to the racism we encounter here; it's something we learn. I learned to understand racism. I was not aware of it in Jamaica. My senses were heightened to the fact that we were being treated as inferior people and second class.

My husband on the other hand was used to these things. He grew up here and experienced racism first-hand. He explained that in his school, they were called "N-----" and beaten. And so it became part of life as they dealt with it constantly.

We did not grow up in such an environment. There was inbred discrimination in the Caribbean due to things like skin colour, even within families, which is more like giving preferential treatment to one over the other.

I would like people outside of our culture to understand that being Black, we are a proud and ambitious people. I think sometimes people think we just want handouts or we want to be like them and that really bugs me. Martin Luther King said judge people by their character and not by the colour of their skin.

It was not my decision to come to Canada, but if I had to choose, I definitely would choose to live in Canada.

ANGELA JOHNSON

Found her doorway to the world

At the age of 14 years, Angela Johnson, her father, and four siblings left the warm shores of Jamaica and headed to the United Kingdom (UK) in search of "greener pastures". Her mother and one of her brothers remained in Jamaica. That experience became the turning point in Angela's life as it became her doorway to the world.

Angela completed her education in the UK and started her career at the Central Criminal Court's probation office, where she held various positions. Although she had great accomplishments in her career and forged strong associations with friends, Angela considers the 18 years she lived in UK as somewhat routine.

She found it extremely difficult to acclimatize to the "gloomy" weather conditions. It rained constantly with little or no sunshine in comparison to the tropical Caribbean weather. She also frowned at the living standards of immigrants, many of who could only afford low-cost housing apartments or even lived in attics with limited space. Especially disheartening to her was hearing immigrants' stories about their paraffin heater running out of fuel in the middle of the night during winter.

While in the UK, Angela took the opportunity to visit several countries, including Canada, prior to her move here in 1982. On one of these visits, she was introduced to a horticultural student at the University of Guelph, who eventually became her husband in 1981.

Angela continued to work in the UK while her papers were being processed for her move to Canada. She travelled in between to Saudi Arabia, spending time with her husband who was hired there upon graduating from university. The couple moved back to Canada soon after her application for residency was approved.

"I am a person who is always on the go," says Angela, a fact with which many of her friends would readily agree. On arrival in Canada, she immediately started job hunting and landed a contract position in a government-run mental health institution in downtown Toronto. After working there for some months, Angela applied for and obtained a full-time position with the Ministry of Industry, Trade and Technology (MITT), where she worked initially in the human resources department and then in the deputy minister's office. She later moved to the international marketing branch, where she had the opportunity to travel and, as a result, met people from various walks of life.

Angela believes in equality and respectfully standing up for one's rights. Although she did not experience racism directly, she believes it exists in a subtle manner. The closest that she came to feeling discriminated against was during a situation which occurred when she worked in the HR department at MITT.

She recalls her workstation was moved frequently until she eventually went in one day and found her work area was significantly reduced. At that point she had to take a stand against what she perceived was unfair treatment. After having a "tantrum" and making a comment to the effect that she "might as well be sitting in the hallway", she was called into the office of the HR manager. Fortunately, the manager had witnessed what was happening and offered Angela a promotion to the deputy minister's office.

Angela didn't give much consideration to becoming involved in politics, but her life changed in 1995 when the Mike Harris Government of Ontario closed the Development Corporation, which affected 165-plus employees, including Angela. It was quite traumatic for Angela and her colleagues even though they were given six months notice and severance. That became another turning point in Angela's life, as she subsequently became more involved in politics and civic engagement.

Angela considers herself a very fortunate individual. She looks at her life now and describes it as "never a dull moment". When she lost her job, she was encouraged to apply as one of Canada's volunteers to the 1996 Olympics in Atlanta. Ironically, she received the notification of selection on the last day of work with the Development Corporation.

Her involvement with the community started in 1985, when she visited Carabram, an annual multi-cultural festival in Brampton, Ontario. The festival was founded in 1982 after volunteers from different ethnic communities wanted to organize a festival celebrating diversity and cross-cultural friendship.

Angela immediately joined the United Achievers Club (UAC), which was one of the main organizers of the festival, and her involvement with Carabram remains till today. Her first major assignment was to serve in the kitchen of the Caribbean Pavilion, which was hosted by the UAC. She did not like that area in particular, but she loved the pavilion so much that she did not mind.

The United Achievers Club grew and eventually established the United Achievers' Community Services (UACS), with its primary focus being to provide much-needed services to the community, especially for seniors of Caribbean descent. Angela grew with the organization and served as president of both the UAC and UACS. She is still actively involved in the seniors group and pursues things that will assist in the development and well-being of the organization.

Angela is a recipient of several awards and accolades, including the Peace Medallion from the YMCA for her contribution on the Carabram festival; Brampton's Citizen of the Year in 1998, and a place on the honour roll with the Peel Children's Aid Society. Her passion and commitment for community development is still strong, and she remains actively involved.

DAISY LEWIS

Whether it rains, shines, sleets, or snows

I was excited to come to Canada in the 1980s. Before then, I spent most of my life in Trinidad and Tobago. Coming to Canada was a great opportunity for me because my daughter was already settled, and I had no issues with where to stay or how to navigate upon my arrival.

Canada was such a clean and beautiful place when I landed. It was actually much more beautiful than what I had read or seen on television. I acclimatized very quickly, and I began looking for possibilities to develop myself. This does not mean things went smoothly all the way.

My first work experience was in a cosmetic warehouse, through an employment agency. It was tedious, but with the mercies of God, I survived and even remained with the company for several years before it folded. Another thing I must not fail to mention is that I lived in the then Bramalea area, which later merged to establish the City of Brampton.

I commuted from Bramalea to a nine-hour work shift in Scarborough. People were perplexed at the distance separating the two cities. In addition to the distance, I spent a lot of my wages on transportation, and it was a herculean task getting ready daily, as I had to leave home very early every morning.

My first winter experience was dreadful too. I would spend the entire day out any time it snowed, and as a result, I ended up eating junk food like crackers, sardines, and ice cream for dinner. I would also wear plastic bags in my shoes to keep my feet warm and prevent them from swelling like that of a penguin. Whenever the situation began to overwhelm me, I would apply my version of the postal service motto, "Whether it rains, shines, sleets or snows…" That reassured me and, in no time, I got used to the process and started to integrate into the system and way of life.

I eventually changed my career and attended evening classes to obtain a certificate in home nursing, as it was then called. Its equivalent today is the personal support worker program. This became my new occupation as time went by. I took this step initially to support my family financially, but in the long run, it became a passion for me to assist people. Although I am retired and actively doing Christian ministry work, I also volunteer in a home for mentally and physically challenged individuals, which I truly enjoy.

EARLINE LEWIS

Sacrifices but no regrets

I was born in Jamaica, and it feels just like yesterday I arrived in Canada because I remember vividly everything about my preparation, including what I wore on my trip to Canada. It was on February 18, 1972, a Friday, that I set foot on this soil. The plane took off from Jamaica at 5 p.m. and landed in Toronto at 9 p.m.

I arrived as a visitor. When I received the invitation to come, I did not hesitate to honour it. I remember telling my parents, and their response was, "You ready to go?" I nodded in affirmation.

Although I was quite excited, leaving Jamaica was not easy at all, because I was going to be leaving a year-and-a-half-old child of mine behind. I was not a drinker, but I had to ask the flight attendant for a drink to quell my anxiety. I slept all through the flight and when I woke up, I realized one of the air hostesses had covered me with a blanket.

When I got off the plane and went through customs and immigration, I still felt quite great and was not considering the weather. Minutes later, I went outside and immediately felt a freeze, plus a strong windchill in the atmosphere that almost cracked my entire body. It was biting cold, and I was very skinny at that time. I didn't prepare well enough for the weather. As a matter of fact, I had on a little short dress. At that point, I just wanted to return home. However, my sister and a few family members met me at the arrival lounge.

The next day, I could not wait to get into the streets of Toronto, specifically to buy a coat and boots to keep me warm. Toronto looked very beautiful. I also took the opportunity to visit the famous Honest Ed's, a landmark discount store that was named after its proprietor, Ed Mirvish, who opened the store in 1948 and oversaw its operations for almost 60 years. I recall that it was cold and snowing heavily. My eyes and nose were running profusely, but it was a good experience at the end of the day.

My visitor's visa was for only three weeks, and so we had to come up with a legitimate plan to keep me here. We contacted an immigration lawyer who filled out the application on my behalf for a fee of $25.

I had to appear at the immigration centre in person. When I walked in, the gentleman I met was very nice. We interacted a bit, and then I waited patiently for his decision. I was very uneasy as I watched him writing. My thoughts were very negative. At some point I muttered, "Oh no, he is going to send me home." The man finally put all the documents in a big brown envelope and handed it to me. He said, "As soon as you do your medical, send it in."

I was overwhelmed with joy. With excitement, I went right across the street and jumped on the streetcar with some dance moves. I quickly looked back to see if the man was behind me watching any of that. When I got home, my cousin was there, and so I explained everything that had happened. It was one of my most ecstatic moments as we both cried in each other's arms.

Eventually, I got my work permit, and I landed my first job, which was sorting the donations that people brought in. It was at a place similar to The Salvation Army Thrift Store.

Thereafter, I worked at Dylex, the clothing giants who owned the famous Tip Top Tailors and Fairweather brands. There were predominantly Portuguese and Italian people working there at that time. After working there for a while, a colleague of mine went on a trip, and I had to fill her position. Soon I encountered what I would describe as my first experience of racism. Someone or a group of people tried to sabotage my efforts by hiding one of the major distribution orders in such a way that I would miss shipping. That could be seen as gross incompetence by management, resulting in getting fired.

Although things were sorted out when the order was mysteriously found in the wrong place, it was apparent that someone wanted to spoil my efforts. I encountered other challenges as well. My child eventually left Jamaica to live here, and it became financially tough on me. I knew I had to get my own place.

I recall going to the bank one Friday to seek a loan, and the teller told me that he could only give me $1,000 toward the rent, furniture, and a host of other household things. But then he said to me quietly, "You know what, go to the store and pick out whatever furniture you want, calculate the total, and come back to me. Then I will take care of it."

I have never regretted coming to Canada any day. My kids joined me and kept me going. I thank God for the opportunity and thank him moreso that they are all grown and doing very well. I have some grandchildren too. I cannot complain.

There were times when I had to work late or overtime, and my neighbour, who was white, would watch the kids. Life was so much better then in terms of safety. We even left our doors unlocked several times, when visiting friends or shopping. No one worried about intruders or home invasions. As a matter of fact, everyone in that building looked out for each other.

Often times, people think that when they go abroad things are easy. That is definitely a wrong assumption, if you are starting from scratch. I worked tirelessly through the years, even when I was feeling sick with ear infections, fever, or the flu because I never earned benefits. I wasn't blessed to get paid for sick days like they are blessed now. There was a lot of sacrificing. My son says to me, "Mom, I don't know how you did it. You played the mom and the dad to us all."

LLOYD MCCURVIN

His defense – the Almighty God

My name is Lloyd McCurvin and I am 83 years old [in 2018]. I am originally from Kingston, Jamaica, but I lived in England for many years with my wife and daughter before I started exploring other options for a better life for my family, even though we were quite comfortable in England.

I looked at several countries and Canada was one of the countries that stood out for me in terms of having broader opportunities and a good environment. I was seeking a better future for my daughter and my wife. And so in 1973, we took the bold step and came here.

I did not really encounter any difficulty processing our immigration documents. It was straightforward and very smooth. The only setback we encountered was that I started processing my documents in the fall season, which translated into arriving in the winter. I did not envisage its harshness. The cold was biting to say the least. It was so bad that I will never recommend coming to Canada in the winter to a first-time visitor, or anyone in my position, without the option to return to the country from which they moved. With time, I got used to the weather due to the fact that English weather was not much better.

Before coming to Canada, I trained as an electrician. But I had to go back to school to obtain the supposedly "Canadian experience", which I received by enrolling and graduating from George Brown College. All the while I worked in a factory. But I recall my first job in Canada was construction work. On completion of my studies, I worked in the airport for 27 years as an electrician.

Initially, it was great working in Canada until a period of time when I experienced racism. One of my supervisors did not seem to take a liking to me and tried everything to get me fired. My only defense was the Almighty God, and so I went into prayer mode over the issue. As a result, the tables turned and he was terminated.

Canada is the best country in the world in my opinion. I have visited many other countries, including India, Russia, and the Middle East. This country is relatively peaceful and full of opportunities, which people often take for granted. I am grateful to be here, but I wish I had all of this as a child. United Achievers' Community Services changed my experience later in Canada by giving me the opportunity to be involved in the community as a senior.

Currently, I belong to three community clubs, including United Achievers' Community Services, a seniors club at my church, and a couple's club. I am able to connect and be viewed as a contributor to my community.

VELMA MCCURVIN

There's no going back

In 1961, at the age of 20 years, Velma McCurvin left her hometown of Kingston, Jamaica, to join her husband in the United Kingdom (UK). The couple's decision to emigrate was primarily in search of a better life.

Although things were much better in England than in Jamaica, Velma missed her family back home greatly, and she would cry every night at the thought of them. While they were in the United Kingdom, Velma and her husband continued their search for a life better than what they were experiencing. They had a daughter who was growing fast, and so they needed a more conducive environment for her growth and development.

Velma and her family spent 11 years in the UK before they eventually left for Canada. Her husband did all the research. He was anxious to ensure their daughter had what she needed to succeed in life, such as a good education and a sound upbringing. He completed the application and followed through with the process. At that time, the procedure was not complicated. It was based on merit points to qualify. As soon as their application was approved, Velma and her family left the UK and arrived in Canada after 10 days of sailing.

Velma and her family were very delighted on their arrival in Montreal. She looked at the land and said to herself, "This is it...no going back." Montreal was not their final destination though, and so they immediately boarded a train to Toronto. They were met by her husband's brother, who was already living there. Velma's older sister was also residing in Toronto, and so settling down was not a tedious task. As a matter of fact, Velma's brother-in-law got them their own accommodation.

Velma's sister assisted her in getting a job at the place she was working. Later, Velma worked with an insurance firm before joining the Provincial Government, where she worked until retirement.

Velma loves Canada. In comparison to the United Kingdom, she finds Canadians warm and friendlier. She noted that in the UK there was prejudice, and people did not hide their feelings about Blacks coming to live there. Velma remembers incidents where Black folks were called derogatory names openly. And some went as far as urging them to go back to their zoo or jungle. There was visible hate and discrimination, such that whenever Blacks wanted to rent apartments, they would be told it had been taken, even though that was not the case. The same treatment applied in many areas in term of jobs.

As cold as the Canadian winter is, Velma and her family prefer it to the "damp and grey" weather of England. It rained almost around the clock during their many years of stay. She is of the opinion, though, that weather conditions may have improved with global warming in effect.

Velma has no regrets whatsoever about coming to Canada. "Not even one regret," she says to everyone.

MARGARET MILLINGTON

Perseverance plus faith in God

When Margaret Millington received the opportunity to immigrate to Canada from Montego Bay, Jamaica, there was no hesitation. She wanted to see what living in another country was like and to broaden her horizons. Therefore, she gladly accepted the opportunity. She received sponsorship and left her family behind, including two children. Her plan was to complete the paperwork for her two children so that they could join her in Canada as soon as she was established. That goal was achieved approximately one year after she arrived in Toronto.

"I remember landing at Pearson International Airport in February 1984, all dressed down in my best clothes," she says. "But I quickly realized it was not suitable attire for a Canadian winter."

Fortunately, the individuals that sponsored her helped her to get acclimatized to winter quickly. Margaret was finally at home in Canada, a place that she had visited on vacation two years before.

Margaret came from very humble beginnings. She was the middle of three children and inquisitive. She became the breadwinner at a young age due to her mother's illness. She loved English as a child and states that she also has a God-given talent for numbers. That love for numbers landed her a career in finance in Jamaica.

However, she faced a stumbling block when she came to Canada. She thought that you just looked for a job, applied and started working. That was not the case. She sought jobs in finance, but was always met with the response, "You need Canadian experience."

But Margaret is a hard worker and diligent. She was taught that no work was degrading as long as it was honest. She realized that she just needed to get a job, and it didn't matter where. She asked around and met someone who worked at Wendy's. Margaret was hired and worked two hours per day, Monday through Friday for $2.75 an hour. She was promoted a few weeks after she started when her manager noticed her gift for numbers. Some of her co-workers didn't like that, but Margaret's hard work and positive attitude were noticed and paid off. She eventually moved on to Arby's where she was paid more money.

Margaret didn't really miss Jamaica. Living in Montego Bay, people bought and sold North American goods there. It was also a hot tourist spot, so there was a constant flow of tourists from North America.

Her children came to join her in Canada approximately one year after she arrived. She was fortunate to settle into an area with a great Caribbean population. They lived in the same neighbourhood, shopped at the same stores, and looked out for each other's children. She actually met some people that were originally from Montego Bay. These things helped her to feel more at home.

Margaret believes that education is the key to success, and she instilled that in her children. She told them that a mind is a terrible thing to waste. "My house was like a library. I bought my kids lots of books, and they had to spend time daily reading and studying," states Margaret. Her diligence paid off. All of her children studied at post-secondary institutions and are gainfully employed in their fields of study.

Margaret upgraded her credentials in order to improve her career chances. Upon completing her courses, she was blessed with a co-op position at a major bank, working three days a week. She was eventually hired by them. Eight years after arriving in Canada, Margaret was back in her element in finance.

"I started as a teller and was promoted to several different positions, including team leader, throughout my career," Margaret says. She always worked on the frontline. She worked at four different branches and became a household name with her customers, who would ask for her by name.

She would encourage her clients to save their money and invest in RESPs and TFSAs, and she shared other tips she knew would benefit them. Due to her pleasant, professional, and caring attitude, she was regularly chosen to represent her branch at meetings at head office where she had the opportunity to socialize with the CEO. After working for 25 years at the bank, Margaret retired in 2017.

She knows that moving to Canada was the right decision. Things were getting tough in Jamaica when she left. To her, Canada is like paradise. She found lots of opportunities here because she inquired and sought them. She faced many struggles and challenges too, including poverty and sickness, but she survived and persevered. She achieved much because she put her mind to it.

Margaret is very kind and humble, has a giving heart, and expresses a lot of gratitude. She believes in giving others your best and would readily give a person the clothes off her back. She often buys items and packs barrels to send home to Jamaica. She will never forget where she came from.

Margaret is an active member in her church, Central Park Baptist Church, and she assists in the hospitality and finance departments. She also had a knack for fundraising.

Margaret gives God all of the glory and says that everything she is and has is through Him. Her favourite Bible verse is Psalm 27:14. "Wait on the Lord: Be of good courage, and He shall strengthen thine heart."

CARMEN MOODIE

Retired with joy

I was born and raised in Kingston, the capital city of Jamaica. After completing my high school education, I studied nursing and became a registered practical nurse equivalent. I was thrilled with the outcome and wanted more. And so I decided to further my career in nursing.

At that time, my older sister was living in England, and I applied for the registered nursing program over there, through the Ministry of Health, and was fortunate to be selected as a candidate.

It was exciting to go to a foreign land to explore better opportunities at that time, but I left Jamaica with mixed feelings. My mother had passed away in her forties, when my baby sister was only 12. In our culture, the role of a deceased mother passes on to the older female children. However, I had to pursue my education to achieve more than just that.

So off I went to the United Kingdom to study and reunite with my older sister.

I successfully completed the program to become a registered nurse and midwife. Thereafter, I decided to take a break to visit Canada. My intention was to come here for a few years and then return to Jamaica to work and help out financially.

I applied for a job in Canada from the United Kingdom. I was hired and came straight to a job at the General Hospital in Oshawa in 1969. I fell in love with Canada the moment I arrived. I talked about it so much that I enticed two of my siblings to immigrate through my sponsorship, and we are all still here today. In addition, the weather here is quite different from that of the United Kingdom. There, you could go to the cinema in sunny weather and, without warning, it is pouring by the end of the movie. In a nutshell, you always have to go about with your raincoat or umbrella.

I had a few regrets from time to time when I got here. For instance, I did not earn as much wages as I expected, which made it difficult with all the expenses and people I had to take care of. Furthermore, there were very few people from my background at that time, even though I shared a two-bedroom apartment with another Caribbean woman. We shared similar challenges, especially in getting West Indian groceries and having our hair done. I had to learn to commute between Oshawa and Toronto by bus.

In the area where we lived in Oshawa, there were even fewer Black folks than in Toronto. And we got "the funny looks" all the time. But in all fairness, no one made any remarks to us. The only time I witnessed a racist remark was in the hospital when one of our patients made an open statement that he did not want a Black individual to attend to him.

I eventually left Oshawa for Scarborough to shorten the distance between myself and my siblings, who resided in Brampton. Apart from taking the bus and several hours to get to them, telecommunication restrictions were also in effect as a call to Brampton was long distance. Actually, that hastened my decision to move to Brampton.

I cannot end my tale skipping "winter". I can freely state that the wintery conditions were more severe when I came to Canada. There is absolutely nothing now to compare with it. But we learned the dress code very fast and coped like everyone else, dressing in layers to keep warm.

On average, Canada is still number one. Despite all the challenges I face, I would choose this country any day. I am retired with joy and strong enough to still deliver babies.

CHRISTIANAH OLAREWAJU

A rewarding journey

After retiring from the workforce twice, Christianah is now doing what she truly enjoys – taking a big interest in her four grandchildren's lives, going to the gym, spending some time on the computer, and volunteering.

Born in Nigeria, Christianah first came to Canada in 1963 as a student to pursue a degree in sociology at Carleton University in Ottawa, Ontario. At that time, most people from Nigeria were going to England to study, but she wanted to go somewhere different. She was working then at the Ministry of Social Welfare in Zaria, Nigeria, which was headed by a Canadian, which factored into her decision to come here.

Her husband-to-be, who went to England as a student, followed her to Canada. Their first daughter was born in Canada before they headed back to Nigeria via England. During the course of time, Christianah changed her career and went into teaching, eventually becoming a school principal. They had two other children and, at age 55, she retired, as is mandatory in Nigeria. She says that as a school principal she had ample opportunity to become involved in politics but she thought about her family and opted to put them first.

By this time, their eldest child had returned to Canada and she sponsored both of them to come back to Canada.

Coming back as an adult, Christianah had a different perspective of Canada from when she first came as a student. At that time, work experience didn't matter, but when she returned, not having Canadian experience was an issue. Also, she found the number of Canadians (not immigrants) who couldn't read or write mind-boggling. Christianah did not intend to sit around and was soon volunteering at an adult literacy centre as a way to get her foot in the labour market. She also worked at Fat Phil's restaurant in Brampton.

One of the places she volunteered was at Distress Centre Peel and, eventually, Christianah was hired as the volunteer coordinator. She subsequently was promoted to management. She spent 17 years with this organization before retiring for a second time in 2015, when Distress Centre Peel and Telecare Distress Centre Brampton merged to form Spectra Community Support Services. Christianah is also a member of Toastmasters and held the position of vice president, membership, at the Meadowvale chapter in Mississauga.

She found the work at the Distress Centre to be extremely rewarding. She gained so much satisfaction from communicating with those in the community who were depressed, suicidal, had lost hope, and just wanted to find their niche in society.

"This has made me appreciate life even more," says Christianah, "especially when you hear people with no hope or seniors who are victims of fraud, who open up their hearts to you – total strangers."

Christianah's compassion was honed while working as a social welfare officer in the Ministry of Social Welfare in Nigeria, where she took up the cause of child prostitution. Many young girls were being married to older men against their wishes. Sometimes they would run away, but then they couldn't go back home or get married again.

"I became a champion for those girls," she says. "I was even called the officer in charge of wayward children. They were considered outcasts."

Today, seeing young Black men killing each other makes her heart ache. She says not knowing how to stop the senseless acts makes her feel helpless. She believes that family dynamics and the way we are raising our children has a major role to play in the escalating violence we are experiencing.

"I believe that we give our children independence too early," she says. Although she notes that the situation in Nigeria is worsening since 2006, she says that children there are not "given independence" until after they graduate or start to work.

She references the Bible scripture that says, "Spare the rod and spoil the child." However, she quickly states that she is not advocating for people to punish their children. She believes that they need to sit them down and instil in them values such as respect. She gives an example of children addressing their parents by their first name, which doesn't sit well with her.

"There are so many areas that need fixing, it is difficult to know where to start," says Christianah. "Many of our young women are raising too many kids, and they are missing out on life. Black youth are being incarcerated for minor offences. They have to assert themselves, they need to get an education, they need to find that desire to achieve," she adds.

Christianah has enjoyed the experiences of her life's journey and says that if she had to travel that way again she would do so with a few improvements.

JOY OSBOURNE

Rising from the shadows

For eight years I lived and worked in the shadows, closely guarding two secrets.

I first came to Canada in 1971 at the invitation of one of my 10 brothers. Growing up in a family with 13 kids meant that there was always someone around, and that you looked after one another. I only stayed for three weeks at that time, but I came back for good in 1972.

My brother helped me to get my first job taking care of children and, from there, I signed up with an agency that sent me to different homes to care for families for short periods of time. In addition, I found other jobs babysitting, cleaning homes, and doing factory work. All the while, I saved as much as I could and sent money to my mother to care for my two children.

It was hard work, and I wasn't making much progress toward the "better life" that I had dreamed about when I first came, so I decided to go back to school.

My first secret was that I couldn't read or write when I came to Canada. School in Jamaica was a terrible experience for me. I didn't understand the lessons, and my attendance was poor because my mother needed my help to care for my eight younger siblings.

Classes in Canada were different. They were fun, and you met people who cared about you and wanted to help. For the first time in my life, I felt like I was learning something instead of going to warm the bench. At the end of my literacy course, I was about to sign up again because I didn't feel ready, but my teacher told me that I was ready to go. No one knew that I was taking these classes. I did it for me, and it gave me confidence to deal with an even bigger issue.

My second secret was that I was living in Canada illegally. In 1972, I slipped in and stayed under the radar, working hard and avoiding any kind of official authority. My employer at that time was a lawyer, and I finally worked up the courage to ask for his help. I told him, "I'm here illegally and I can't take it anymore." He looked at me and asked why I didn't tell him sooner, and then he called a friend who was an immigration lawyer. I had my landed immigrant status within six months, which paved the way for me to visit Jamaica for the first time since I had left and to bring my kids to Canada.

My first trip back to Jamaica was when I knew that Canada had become my home. I could barely understand my own kids. Here, I worked with many different families and was exposed to different ways of thinking, eating and having fun.

I love the cold! I used to love taking the kids I worked with to go skating or tobogganing, or just being outside to play in the snow. I wanted the same for my children.

They were young teenagers when they came to Canada. It was hard for them because they grew up in one system and were very accustomed to how things worked, but here it was completely different. However, they both went on to do well in school and graduate from post-secondary programs. I'm proud of the small part that I played in helping them to create that success.

I love Canada because I can go anywhere. After living in the shadows, I appreciate the freedom and opportunity that is everywhere in Canada.

BEVERLY SAMUELS

Stepped out in faith

On August 23, 1972, Beverly Samuels left Clarendon, Jamaica and headed to Canada with her aunt. They settled in Toronto, but she ended up moving in with a friend and her mother. She had actually planned to move to the United States because she had family there. About one month prior to her departure, she was urged by her father to go to Canada instead. He felt that she knew the aunt who was moving here much better than her other family members.

She had never travelled abroad prior to coming to Canada. She had heard good things about Canada. It was a land full of opportunities and; back then, it wasn't as "racist as America".

Upon arrival, Beverly went to immigration, applied for her Social Insurance Number, and began to work as soon as it arrived. She wasn't fussy about the type of work. As far as she was concerned, a job was a job. She secured a job in a factory making toothbrushes, which paid fairly well.

In the early years, Beverly experienced sadness at times due to home-sickness and because she missed her young children. She was blessed to have a wonderful best friend who shared a similar plight. Her friend was missing England from where she had recently immigrated. They would chat, cry and share memories together of their beloved homeland, Jamaica. Her friend encouraged her to stay, and they stuck it out together.

Although Beverly was never the direct recipient of racism, she recalls a time when she witnessed blatant discrimination. She was living in Toronto in a home with two white female roommates. They went to a bar, and she noticed a Black couple was being turned away. Beverly felt she was given a "pass" because she was with two white girls. She immediately moved out of that home and area.

Beverly held several jobs in Canada, including working at a pharmaceutical company and as a travel consultant. Her children came to join her in Canada four years after she left Jamaica. In 2000, she started working at an agency as a personal support worker.

She was asked if she wanted to do a full weekend shift, which meant that she had to sleep over. Her initial response was "no". She didn't want to sleep over at anyone's house. Her manager kept asking her about it and encouraged her to take the shift. It was at the home of a prominent Toronto lawyer. Eventually she agreed, and it turned out to be one of the best decisions that she made.

Beverly arrived at the home and was warmly greeted by a woman who asked her if she wanted some breakfast, to which she replied "no thanks". The woman told her it was nonsense and prepared breakfast for her. They chatted and got to know each other.

Beverly was hired to be the caretaker for the former nanny of the lawyer's now adult children. The lawyer cared so much for their Jamaican nanny that the nanny became a part of their family. The lawyer had vowed to take care of her when she got old and renovated their home to make living quarters for her in her latter years.

Beverly took wonderful care of the nanny, and her friendship with the lawyer and her family grew. Little did she know that her employer had a vision for her. The lawyer would repeatedly ask her if she knew any personal support workers looking for work. Beverly kept replying "no".

The lawyer said to her one day after about one year on the job that she was smart enough to run her own business. Beverly was so inspired and encouraged by the lawyer's confidence in her that she went and registered her business. Entrepreneurship was in her blood. Her father was a butcher, and she had owned a grocery store in Jamaica. In fact, she was selling ice and snow cones at the age of 11.

The lawyer was an immediate and constant source of referrals, so Beverly's business was successful from the beginning. She also took care of the lawyer and her husband during their last days. Her client base includes lawyers, judges and various other professionals. She is blessed to have received the opportunity and has been running a successful business since then with approximately 40 employees – most of whom have worked for her for over a decade.

Though she is past retirement age, she loves what she does. She manages her business, enjoys life and loves travelling.

Beverly is happy that she moved to Canada. She would not go back to Jamaica to live, but she visits family. “I know what it’s like to need a dollar, have a dollar, and to have no needs or worries. I’m in a good place, and I live a good life. I’m blessed.”

DOROTHY SAMUELS

Determined to learn fast

I arrived in Canada on July 17, 1963. I thought it was the most beautiful country I had ever seen. But I must admit that my first winter experience was a great shock to me. The first snowstorm came the first week of December. No one had told me about snowstorms and the chills of the winter season.

Furthermore, the accessories for the season were most uncomfortable. The coats were heavy, and boots took a while to get used to. As a matter of fact, I slipped and fell at least four times that season. But I was determined to learn fast, especially when I started feeling the cold in my bones.

After a year of domestic internship, I started searching for a job and accommodation. During that period, it was extremely hard finding adequate housing to rent. Most of us who came from the Caribbean found it difficult to get an apartment. I personally experienced going to places where landlords had vacant apartments, and they said to me that they were taken. I could see from their looks that my colour and cultural orientation were barriers. I went back few months later and the apartments were still unoccupied.

In the long run, we rented rooms through a club that was formed by established people from the West Indies. We met Fridays and Saturday nights, and it was such a good place to relax and forget our hardships.

At that time, Caribbean women outnumbered men, as men were not given the same opportunity to come live here. Therefore, many of the women who completed the [West Indian] Domestic Scheme sponsored their spouses. It was very exciting finding somewhere to go and being able to relate with others from similar cultures. It was then that I decided I was going to remain here. My mental state of mind improved tremendously as a result of this experience. Loneliness fast disappeared, and things got much better when my family started growing.

EGLON SEALY

Building on the decision his mother made

He didn't have a say in the decision to immigrate to Canada, but Eglon (Lon) Sealy, believing his mother knew what was best for the family, took it in stride and has since forged a path that took him places beyond his dreams.

In November 1964, he, his mother, and his sister, left Barbados for Montreal to join his eldest brother who was on a scholarship at McGill University. One other brother stayed in Barbados but joined them a few years later. Ironically, his brother who was at McGill returned to Barbados and left them here.

They had some relatives living in Montreal who had secured a place for them to live as his brother was living on campus. It soon became apparent that serious decisions needed to be made regarding their financial situation and future, and Lon was the one to take charge. He knew little about Canada and even less about Montreal, except that it was in French-speaking Quebec.

Lon's mother didn't work in Barbados. His father, who was the engineer and manager at Joe's River Sugar Facility, died when he was three years old and his sister was just months old. On completing high school in Barbados, Lon worked for a short while in the Ministry of Agriculture before leaving for Canada. His passport listed his occupation as "lab technician", but to work in that capacity in Canada, you needed a degree which wasn't a requirement in Barbados. He had to find a job and continue his education at the same time.

The employment centre sent him to the Jewish General Hospital where he was hired as an orderly on the night shift (from 11 p.m. to 7 a.m.). This allowed him to go to school full-time at Aviron Technical Institute, where he graduated with a diploma in mechanical design. He then enrolled at Loyola College in the three-year industrial engineering program. He wanted to be a lawyer, but his mother and eldest brother felt he should follow in his father's footsteps and continue in the engineering profession.

Life in Montreal was vastly different from Barbados, especially in the 1960s, with the various political, economic, and social movements occurring around the world. When Lon left Barbados, the political winds were just beginning to change course throughout the Caribbean.

The attempt at a West Indian federation had failed, and the sovereign nations were seeking their own independence from Britain. Two years after he left, Barbados gained its independence, following Jamaica and the twin-island state of Trinidad and Tobago. In 1962, the Barbados government made free education compulsory for every child up to the age of 16 years, removing the barriers that tied higher education to wealth.

The Civil Rights and Black Power movements in the United States were at their peak, and in Quebec, the French were seeking more decision-making power in Canada amidst talks of separation. He recalls the French referring to themselves as *Les Nègres blancs d'Amérique*[10] (translated *The White Negroes of America*) taken from the book written by Pierre Vallières, a leader in Front de libération du Québec.

That decade ended with the unrest at Sir George Williams University (now Concordia University), which saw a number of students being arrested for $2 million of damage to computer equipment. This had followed a students' protest of the university administration's decision regarding a complaint of racism that had been filed several months earlier by six Black students from the Caribbean.[11]

For a young man from a small island with a predominately Black population, living in Montreal during that period was

---

10 Les Nègres blancs d'Amérique is a work of non-fiction literature written by Pierre Vallières, a leader of the Front de libération du Québec

11 "The Sir George Williams Affair" published in the Canadian Encyclopedia. Retrieved from https://www.thecanadianencyclopedia.ca/en/article/sir-george-williams-affair.

bewildering, challenging, and yet exciting. Lon was forced to confront his Blackness in his interactions with other West Indians living in Montreal as well as with Canadians and visiting Americans.

Lon knew he was Black, and there were black and white issues in Barbados, but he never considered Barbados to be racist until he met his Jamaican, Trinidadian and Guyanese counterparts in Montreal. This puzzled him for some time.

He also had the opportunity to meet some of the leading figures in the Black Power movement from the US. He was "awakened" by their depth of knowledge,. He was captivated by the Black Muslims and their fight for better conditions for Blacks. For a time, he was caught up in the movement and was actually recruited by a group headed by Ella Little-Collins, the sister of Malcolm X who had taken over his leadership role after his assassination.

On graduating from Loyola College, Lon was hired by a contracting firm, Roberts Ltd, where he was quickly promoted to chief designer. At that time, employers would go to a school to select the graduates with top marks for their firms.

This was the beginning of a career that took Lon across Canada and worldwide. He spent eight years with Roberts working throughout Quebec before joining SNC-Lavalin as a project cost engineer and senior cost estimator. This move provided him with a broader perspective of engineering in various industries such as nuclear energy, pulp and paper, mining, solar, wind, oil and gas, and power generation.

With this depth of knowledge and expertise, both domestic and foreign, Lon was sought after in the field. This is evident by the various companies where he was employed and the countries in which he worked. He continued his education, gaining certification in project management and quantity surveying.

At SNC-Lavalin, he was seconded to work with Atomic Energy of Canada (AECL) in the nuclear field, which took him to China, Japan and Korea. He worked at Davy McKee, where he spent some time in Russia; Fluor Daniel Canada Ltd, where he worked in California and Vancouver; TransAlta Energy and First Solar Electric Co., which took him to Sarnia, Ontario, and Vale Inc., in Sudbury, Ontario, among others.

Although he is retired, Lon still consults for many local and foreign companies in leadership and mentoring roles. He attributes his success to his upbringing in Barbados, his close-knit family life, and the continuous pursuit of education.

He has no regrets about his life in Canada and the decision his mother made, although she seemed to have regretted the move in the early days. However, when he returns to Barbados and sees the healthy and happy lifestyle that some of his childhood friends attained, he wonders what his life would have been like if he had stayed. He enjoys the ability to travel back and forth between the two countries but feels that after spending the majority of his life in Canada, he would find Barbados too confining to live there.

Lon has witnessed many changes since 1964. The demographics have changed dramatically with the arrival of immigrants from all over the world. Work requirements have changed and even obtaining citizenship has changed.

What causes him some concern is the limited number of Black youth going into scientific and technological fields.

"I find that as Blacks we continue to miss the opportunity to leave our footprints in Canada," he says. "We have not established ourselves as a strong economical or political force in Canada. We brought our old habits with us to Canada. I have lived in Montreal, Vancouver and Toronto among other West Indians, and we seem to stay in the same West Indian mentality as back home."

Lon says that the community needs to develop strong leaders that are not inhibited by the past but rather have the foresight to grasp the full perspective of Canada and where it is heading.

"We know there is a shortage of skills in engineering and digital technology, but we are not steering our kids in that direction," he says. "We need to get our kids involved at an early age. There is a need for people like me to get out there to reach the young children, and that is now my focus."

VINNETTE SINCLAIR

I knew things would get better

I was born and grew up in Jamaica until the age of 16, when my sister who was living in Canada since 1969 sponsored me. I arrived in 1971. It was a very exciting and overwhelming period, but because I was quite young, only 16, I focused more on the childish things like the infrastructure and the weather. I immediately noticed it was cleaner here than it was in Jamaica in terms of sanitation. And it snowed, which was a new experience.

My first job was at McDonald's on Avenue Road in Toronto, and I earned a $1.75 an hour. I was happy enough and did not have many difficulties settling down. The only struggles we had at that time was with finances. We had limited cash flow since my sister had sponsored me, and I was not qualified for any social assistance. As a matter of fact, she was responsible for my care for a ten-year period, according to the sponsorship agreement. But I worked and went to school at the same time to reduce her burden.

I had every opportunity to work as a house cleaner and make lots of money, but I chose to be law-abiding and worked at McDonald's because that was one of the few places you could work under the age of 18.

When I reflect on those days, I see that so many changes have taken place since then. Even with the weather, you can definitely see a distinction. We had freezing rain as early as September, but today the earliest you normally see that is December. Also, we have more opportunities today in terms of financial growth. We could not even obtain a credit card at that time. All you had was the wages you earned. You could not invest in any business. The financial institutions would not trust us enough to give loans for investments. You can imagine how long it would take for the dream of owning a house to materialize.

Overall, I was happy and did not miss Jamaica much. As a matter of fact, my sister eventually sponsored my mother and that made me feel very much at home. The one thing I miss though is the sunshine, and that thought occurs whenever winter sets in.

I have heard people talk so much about racism, segregation and discrimination, but in all honesty, I did not experience anything like what they talked about. Perhaps it was because I was young and my academic pursuit was my primary aim. I went to work in the day and went to school at night. I received some government allowance for transportation when I furthered my education and training. With such assistance, I was able to attend Humber College.

At Humber College, I did not experience racism at all. There was a mix of Black cultures from the various Caribbean islands and some African countries. As a result, I did not feel left out.

I did most of my growing up here, and as soon as I had my first child, I made the decision to stay permanently. I believe that living in Canada is a better choice than living in Jamaica owing to the fact that you are almost certain to attain success if you do the right things here. Whereas at the age I left Jamaica, it was the right age to begin hanging around people who could have influenced me negatively. Life here is structured, and I have no regrets whatsoever about coming to live here.

Things rapidly changed over time, especially with our financial situation. At some point, we were allowed to obtain credit cards. Normally, only the elite whose income can pay it off or had a good record had such privileges. In the past, some people of colour borrowed money, but it was from private companies similar to the cash money businesses of today. I remember my brother-in-law went to a Portuguese merchant who was also a lender when he wanted a down payment towards the property he was looking to acquire.

I also bought a home later on, but I recall approaching the banks between 1989 and 1990, and I was turned down even though I thought I had a good bank account. The bank manager looked at me and said, "You cannot buy a house because your income is insufficient to pay for it."

I remained very optimistic, knowing that things would get better here with time.

YVONNE STAFFORD

Follow your dreams

Yvonne was born in Jamaica, but she lived for about 38 years in the Bahamas. Her journey out of Jamaica began when her sister emigrated with her husband who was in the police force. At that time, the Bahamas recruited professionals from other Caribbean islands.

Yvonne embarked on a few trips to visit her sister before finally making the decision to live there. In fact, her decision to live in the Bahamas for the period she refers to as "most of her young life" was influenced by "the man of her dreams", during one of her visits. Both of them were pretty young then.

Yvonne felt at home in the Bahamas even though she quickly realized the people were envious of Jamaicans. They were jealous of the progressive nature of Jamaicans, who increasingly became connected and operated in the corridors of power. The Jamaicans were in all affairs, and Yvonne was not left out.

She became a citizen and attained her first job with the Royal Bank. After ten years of service, she took a leap of faith and moved into the airline industry. People thought it was a risky decision not because she was moving from one industry to a completely different one, but rather that the former was a full-time position, while the latter was a contract job.

The airline industry was Yvonne's passion. She recalls how she became involved. A customer of hers who worked in the airline industry came to her workplace, and Yvonne expressed her desire to work with them, should there be an opening. A few weeks later, she was informed there was a posting for a vacant position and she should apply, which she did.

Yvonne not only became full-time three weeks after she started work with the US-based airline carrier, she spent 15 years with the company, ending in a managerial position.

In 1991, Yvonne and her family decided to move to Canada. It seemed like another drastic decision to the people around them. They thought she had a good job and her family was well established. But Yvonne was hearing something different from God. She loved the Bahamas, but she was planning for her children's future as well. She believed Canada was a better place to raise and integrate them.

When she and her family arrived in Canada, Yvonne found it quite nice. It was the month of May, and everything seemed to be going well. But like many other immigrants, she found something different instantly. She was overwhelmed with the multicultural way of life. There were white, Chinese, Portuguese, Italian, and a few African and Caribbean people, whereas 95 per cent of the population in the Bahamas was Black. She found that people of the different cultures in Canada identified with their own groups and did not want to mix too much with others.

Since she could not fit in any other culture, Yvonne started searching for a Caribbean culture club. Fortunately, she found one, the United Achievers Club. She joined immediately and has been with the organization since then.

Within 10 days of arriving in Canada, she was hired by the Toronto Dominion Bank at a relatively lower position than her previous position as airline manager. She and her spouse had four children, and so they had to start with something to enable then to gain "Canadian experience". But her passion was in travel, and so she spent nine years at the bank during which time she went back to school to study travel agency management.

Yvonne spent two years in the travel program. As soon as her course wrapped up, all the other students except Yvonne got placement. It became the turning point for Yvonne. As a matter of fact, it was her first time experiencing discrimination. The other time would be when her kids were denied job application forms, and then her husband who is white went in, and he was given the forms.

Their family strategy was to raise their kids to be determined, to learn every good thing as much as possible, and never allow the colour of their skin to determine who they are and what they can accomplish.

Yvonne is a very determined woman yet full of humility. She holds on to her Creator who provides and supplies everything to cover her needs. When a door closes, she starts looking for the opening of another. So she bypassed the institution and started applying for jobs in newspaper ads by faith. She found favour and landed in Travel Choice Express, one of Ontario's largest travel consulting firms.

Although she had some travel skills from her past experience, Yvonne did not have all that was required for the position. She had major concerns after leaving the interview session. Apart from the skills she lacked, she did not see any diversity among the staff. But Yvonne loved the environment and recalls asking God to grant her the position. A week later, she received a call from the manager, who said to her, "I've done my interviewing and have decided to go with you. Although you do not have any experience in this region of travel, with your past experience, I am going to give you a try."

Yvonne is a fast learner. She ended up working in the business development section without much knowledge of the procedures. She relied on the manuals (three books), and so she quickly developed a strategic plan that was a success.

In all her Canadian work experiences, Yvonne recalls she was the only Black on the frontline. She owes her uniqueness to her passion to help people and to accomplish tasks with excellence. She is truly a community woman. She served on the Carabram (an annual multicultural festival in Brampton, Ontario) board and, even in her retirement, she is still involved.

JOSEPHINE STEWART

Doing what needs to be done

I was born and raised in Jamaica. Leaving the Caribbean to settle in a country like Canada was not a desire for me. In comparison to the Caribbean tropical weather, Canada is extremely cold, especially in the winter. Nevertheless, I ended up here in the spring of 1973. It was on May 23rd to be precise.

My parents and brothers were already living in Canada, under my uncle's sponsorship. As a matter of fact, I was eligible to come over when the rest of my folks emigrated, but the weather just wasn't for me. Moreover, I had two kids, who were top of my priority list, and so I thought I should stay behind and raise them in Jamaica.

I can say that my decision to immigrate to Canada was somewhat as a result of being lonely. At some point, I looked around me and realized that I was technically alone, even though I had my immediate family, comprising a husband

and two children. Everyone else was living a distance – geographically – from home. I was becoming anxious, and so I asked my dad to sponsor me, since the initial invitation I received had expired.

When I arrived, everything was pretty straightforward because most of my family members were already here. Settling down was not difficult for me. I found a job as a healthcare aid, which is known today as personal support worker (PSW). We had to take some courses to upgrade our proficiency. To get into that field was not difficult. I had an aunt who worked in a nursing home and she made the necessary connections. I was actually interested in nursing while I was in Jamaica, but I did not pursue it there.

My work experience was great. My first manager was a very approachable person and so the work environment was quite warm. I worked with that same organization, in the same location, for 41 years. I experienced different situations and changes in management and acquisitions. When another company bought the organization, they retained us as their staff. The field gave Black folks a lot of job security, and so I cashed in and adapted to all subsequent changes.

I just went in and did what needed to be done. You have to like what you do. If you don't, it's just a paycheque. Many times, I told people "the job didn't choose me, I chose the job". I worked eight-hour nights for 41 years (11 p.m. to 7 a.m.).

Things were rough at first with three young children. Where we resided was half a mile from their school, and there was no school bus. I had to come in from overnight shift, get them ready and walk them to school.

Kindergarten ran up till 11.30 a.m., and I would have to go back again to pick them up. Occasionally, a friend would volunteer to take them to enable me to get some sleep. My main sleep time was from 6 p.m. to 10 p.m.

My husband and I wanted someone to be home with the kids at all times. He worked days and I worked nights, and so they were lucky they did not have to go to babysitters. All of that would have been taken care of if we had remained in Jamaica. It is cultural for families or folks in the community to join hands and assist with things like childcare and in raising children.

I also did some part-time driving. I used to drive buses at the airport. I drove for the Pacific Bus Company for awhile, and sometimes I transported people down to Toronto. I had a very busy life in the past, but I am retired and relaxing these days.

Canada is very different from Jamaica in terms of opportunity. I am glad I made the decision to live here. I can imagine how difficult it would have been raising my kids in Jamaica. At high-school age, I would have struggled to financially support them. In fact, I may not have sent them at all. I am pleased with our decision to live here. If I were given the opportunity to choose again, I will definitely choose to live in Canada.

MARJORIE TAYLOR

An attitude of gratitude

"My philosophy is to help others; I believe in giving back," says Marjorie Taylor, who can be found on any day volunteering around the City of Brampton where she resides.

When she is not at the Christ Church Anglican Church at choir practice, singing on Sundays, or serving on the Altar Guild or as a Eucharistic lay assistant, you may find her at the United Achievers Club preparing for the annual scholarship awards or the Celebrity Chefs Who Cook and breakfast fundraisers. Maybe you will find her volunteering with the Kiwanis Club, attending a meeting of the Region of Peel Black Advisory Committee or the William Osler Patient and Family Advisory Council. You may also see her going door-to-door canvassing for the Canadian Cancer Society, something she has done for over 25 years.

This dynamo mother of three believes in lifelong learning, and so it's no surprise that education was a driving factor in her decision to immigrate to Canada. Holding the position of number four in a family of seven children, Marjorie was raised in the parish of Westmoreland, Jamaica. Her mother encouraged and facilitated them to go to high school. But her father died when she was 10 years old and there wasn't sufficient money for everyone to pursue post-secondary education.

Her eldest sister studied nursing in Jamaica and immigrated to Canada. Her two elder brothers both received scholarships – one to study in Alberta and the other in New York. Her mother then took an opportunity to immigrate to the United States and was able to take the three youngest children with her.

On completing high school, Marjorie worked as a student teacher, in the parish library in Montego Bay, and at a gas company in Kingston before her sister sponsored her to come to Canada. She saw this as her ticket to further her education, and in November 1969, she arrived in Canada and went to live with her sister in East York.

She immediately sought a job, as she did not want to be a burden to her sister. She was fortunate to secure a position at the Metropolitan Toronto Library, where she worked until 1986. She also enrolled in the human resources program at Ryerson Polytechnic (now Ryerson University).

During that time, Marjorie was somewhat "side-tracked", as she puts it: she fell in love, married and became mother to three beautiful sons. In 1981, she moved to Brampton with her husband who was offered a position there. However, the marriage faltered and they divorced.

After her divorce, she made some calculated decisions about her future. She knew it wouldn't be easy being a single mother, but she knew she wanted to accomplish some things, and she set out on the path to achieve them.

She left the library and took up a position at Women's College as an administrative assistant, commuting from Brampton to Toronto until the year 2000, when she had the opportunity to work closer to home at Peel Memorial Hospital. She retired from there in 2007.

It wasn't an easy road that she travelled, especially when one of her sons was diagnosed with leukemia and another with asthma. But her deep faith in God and her belief in helping others no matter how insignificant it may seem have proven to be pillars of comfort. As well, she is someone who is proactive, and she learned all she could about these illnesses to ensure her children were well cared for under the circumstances.

Throughout the years, Marjorie has been able to combine her two passions well – education and volunteerism – at work and in the community.

In Jamaica, she was a Guides Ranger. She also sang in the choir, played netball, participated in athletics, and even performed in plays. Soon after arriving in Brampton, she joined Christ Church and immediately become involved with the activities there.

When her youngest son was 13 years old, Marjorie went back to school and graduated from Wycliffe College with a Diploma in Lay Ministry.

She believes that the life skills she acquired from Jamaica and honed in Canada through her continuous learning – formally and informally – have enabled her to develop leadership qualities that have served her well.

"You have to be aware of what is happening around you. You see how people operate, and you take your cues from them," she says, adding that she gravitates to what is best around her.

While not experiencing overt racism and prejudice, Marjorie feels that systemic racism is prevalent, which is hard to fight because it is institutionalized. She is sympathetic to the needs of Black children and youth, especially those who are born in Canada. She is a strong advocate for Black youth to help them rise above the fray and to manoeuvre the institutionalized racism they have to navigate.

Marjorie's selfless contributions have not gone unnoticed, as she has received many accolades over the years for the service she bestows on others. These include the Mission Marathon Award from the Women's College Hospital for staff going above and beyond the call of duty; a finalist for the Zonta Women of Achievement Awards (November 2007); the Kiwanis Club of Brampton Community Service Award (2009); United Achievers Club Member of the Year Award (2001, 2002, 2006); Spelling Bee of Canada Certificate of Recognition (2008); Helping Hands for Good Certificate of Recognition (2012); the Ontario Government Volunteer Recognition Award for community service; Canadian Cancer Society Certificate of Recognition for 20 years of service; the Queen's Diamond Jubilee Medal (October 2012); the H. Franklin Parker Award in recognition for "extraordinary service and dedication to the community" (2014), and the 2015 Brampton Citizen of the Year Award.

"I live intentionally each day, and I am thankful," says Marjorie. "I continue to have an attitude of gratitude, and I find life very rewarding. I have gone through challenges, which have strengthened me. There are challenges from time to time, but with God's help, friends, and family, we can overcome them."

ELAINE WALCOTT

Thankful for the opportunity

Elaine Walcott came to Canada from Jamaica in 1967 at the invitation of family friends who needed assistance with their kids. At that time, it was easy for people from the Caribbean to visit Canada.

Like many visitors, Elaine was originally supposed to visit for two weeks, but she fell in love with the country and ended up overstaying. During that period, she met her spouse and they got married. Soon after, the couple went back to Jamaica for a brief period in order to get acquainted with their various family members.

Although it was not such a difficult process to get into Canada as a visitor, it was much more difficult to become a landed immigrant. Sponsorship was required and, because Elaine had overstayed, she needed the service of an attorney to assist with the process. One was hired and Elaine eventually received her landed immigrant status.

The Canadian winter can be brutally cold, and that was something that stuck in the hearts of immigrants who came to Canada in the 1960s and 1970s. When Elaine encountered her first wintery experience, she describes it as a "deep freeze" that lasted until the month of May. She can see a change in the weather today, whereby temperatures are not only milder but the season is shorter.

Other than the cold weather, things went quite well with Elaine. She explains that one of the reasons she decided to leave Jamaica was that her mother had died, leaving herself and a brother behind with their dad who had another spousal relationship. Everyone around her seemed to have started their own families with their spouses, including her brother. Elaine was beginning to feel like an outsider, and so she decided that she needed to start a life of her own with a husband and children.

Elaine's career goal was to be a registered nurse, and she started her first stint at Sunnybrook Hospital. She remembers how easy it was to get a job in those days. She simply walked to the site, and the hiring manager wanted her to start work on the following day.

When Elaine came to Canada, she saw only a handful of Black folks. As a matter of fact, if you wanted to meet them, you needed to go to Honest Ed's, a landmark for tourists and an entertaining shopping experience for all. Honest Ed's was a one-of-a-kind bargain centre that had almost everything.

Another reason you could not find many Black people was that the opportunity to come to Canada was primarily for women to come in as live-in workers. The women would in turn sponsor their spouses after their contract had ended.

While she worked at her Sunnybrook job, Elaine noted that the majority of staff were very pleasant. They were not only satisfied with her work, but the way she spoke and the manner in which she conducted herself. However, she was not so naïve that she didn't realize some of them were acting. Others were inquisitive, wanting only to obtain information and details about her lifestyle. "That group will normally play around you, but when push comes to shove, they will never be available to back you," she says.

She believes, in general, people were friendlier back then. Racism was there but "swept under the carpet". During her career as a nurse, she recalled some white folks addressing Black people in a derogatory manner, but she associated most of those remarks with the nature of their illness.

Elaine doesn't have any regrets about the years she has spent in Canada. In fact, she loves Canada and is thankful to God for the opportunity to live here.

ALDA WALLACE

Parental discipline was her strength

Alda Wallace credits her strong parental upbringing in Jamaica for giving her the strength to overcome the challenges she encountered after she immigrated to Canada. She arrived in Canada in May 1968, after being sponsored by an older sister. Unfortunately, soon after she arrived, her sister had to leave the country for a short while, and Alda had to fend for herself from the outset.

She was able to obtain a job, which paid $1.35 per hour, and rented a one-room apartment. She recalls how very often she changed jobs, not because she wanted to, but because she was only being hired on a contract basis for short-term assignments.

To survive and improve herself emotionally and financially, Alda realized that she needed to upgrade her skills. She enrolled in night school and then pursued post-secondary studies. She registered for different courses, including mechanics, data processing and computers, and completed the restorative nurse assistant program at Seneca College, where she graduated with honours.

After graduating from college, she was able to secure an office job. Her first assignment was with Sears as a data processing operator. She stayed with that company for 18 years before moving to the Lester B. Pearson Airport, where she worked until 2016.

Like most immigrants from the tropics, Alda found the Canadian winter extremely harsh compared to the constant sunshine in Jamaica. But it was not in Canada that she experienced her first snowfall – it was in New York when she went to visit her brother. During the tough winter months, there were several occasions when she felt like going back to Jamaica to enjoy the freedom of putting on light outfits and basking in the sun somewhere by the beach.

Alda says she did not experience direct racism. "My way of dealing with bigotry was not to take offensive words to heart," she says. "I would rather turn those words into jokes. Actually, people who tried to upset me ended up being my friends," she quips.

Alda is charismatic, yet possesses a lot of self-control, which brings a feeling of peace to many people. She attributes this attitude to the discipline she received from her parents.

She was taught how to behave in public: stay out of peoples' matters or anything that is not addressed toward her. She vividly remembers her parents reminding her always to "see and be blind, hear and be deaf", meaning no matter what you see, seal your lips, and whatever you hear, block your ears.

"I have no regrets living in Canada," says Alda, although she no doubt struggled through some difficult times before achieving success. She is convinced that her present lifestyle far outweighs any struggles of the past.

MILLICENT WALLACE

Blessings in disguise

Millicent Wallace was born in Jamaica on June 14, 1948. As a young child, she had many dreams of getting on an airplane and flying around the world. As she grew older, she became anxious to pursue her dream. The opportunity finally came at the ripe age of 21 and, on September 29, 1969, Millicent boarded an aircraft and left the Caribbean shores on a visitor's visa to Canada.

Like most immigrants, Millicent came to North America with very high expectations. Her dad had passed away a year prior to her departure. She envisaged the journey to Canada as a gateway to better her life and her mother's in Jamaica. But she didn't realize that a visitor did not have the same privileges as a landed immigrant.

As a result, Millicent underwent excessive struggles to make ends meet. She started out in a room-and-board rental system where, in exchange for money, labour or other considerations, a person was provided with a place to live as well as meals on a comprehensive basis.

As a visitor who could not earn regular wages, Millicent became a babysitter and was given "pocket money" to supplement. Out of that money, she sent a portion to her mother. The situation remained unchanged until she got married in 1970. With a companion in her life, things began to ease a bit. They were blessed with a son the following year.

Millicent is a woman of great faith. With all the hardship she experienced, she looks at every encounter as a blessing in disguise. In that regard, she added something else to her pursuit. She enrolled in college to further her education while her son was still a baby. Upon graduating, Millicent secured a position as a healthcare support worker in a retirement home and worked there for 24 years until she retired.

Things improved for Millicent and her family over the years. She had two more children that are now fully grown and supportive. She can also boast of some grandchildren, nephews and nieces in Canada.

She reminisced that in the past, the Caribbean folks who lived in Toronto gathered around Parliament and Bathurst area to socialize. Their meeting point was the famous Honest Ed's, a discount store. It was such a great landmark because most of the items sold were less than a dollar, from which many newcomers benefited.

Like many other Black people, Millicent experienced her fair share of discrimination. At the nursing home where she worked for several years, she and many other Blacks were picked on and constantly watched. She was not gravely disturbed by any of these circumstances though, owing to the fact that she was raised by a preacher father along with nine other children. Their father left them with a legacy of prayer and a belief in God, in spite of any circumstance. That has kept Millicent going over the years, through good and bad times.

Millicent remembers every detail of her departure and arrival into Canada. As much as she suffered and endured a lot, the joyful memories of her successes and her transition from a visitor to a landed immigrant and then to a citizen of Canada is priceless. If it were possible for her to start all over and have the opportunity to choose which country she would prefer to live in, Canada remains her first and only choice.

WILLIAM WEST

"Know Who You Is"

I grew up on a steady diet of wisdom from elders and a pastor – my father. What I didn't know growing up was that one particular refrain would frame many life experiences to come.

I arrived in Canada at Lester B. Pearson in Toronto en route to Montreal's Dorval Airport in September 1975. It was cold like I had never experienced even though I had lived and worked in the United Kingdom for many years before coming here. I pulled my jacket closely around me and thought about the coat that I would buy to deal with the cold. Luckily, I have always had the habit of not trying to change things that I can't, so I knew I had to adapt because the weather wouldn't change.

Being a Black man in Canada in 1975 was eye opening. The same needs that Black men have are the same needs that white men have. The difficulty happens when white men decide to erode the rights of Black men. Understanding this was one of the things that helped me to deal with some of the hardships I faced when I was in Montreal.

I was brought up by my parents in Barbados and especially my grandfather. He would say to me: "Boy, don't left this house and don't know who you is."

Every morning I would put on my shoes and get ready to go to school, and he would say: "Boy, don't left this house and don't know who you is."

I heard that so many times. Finally, one day I asked him what it meant. He called me to his side and pointed outside to my best friend who was playing across the street. "If you don't know who you is here," he explained, "when you get out there with him and his friends, and they tell you come and do something that you know is not right, if you don't know who you are, you will never be able to say to them 'that ain't me.'"

I got it. I understood.

In Montreal, because I knew who I was, I did not accept anybody telling me that I was something else. I was comfortable with who I was so when they would call me "N-----", which they did, it meant nothing. I said to one man once, "What is a N-----?" He looked at me and said, "You." I looked back and said, "I'm not a N-----. With your attitude, you are more of a N---- than I am."

There were some good points and some awful points. I remember facing some real harsh moments and rather than responding, I kept silent. I didn't say anything when people disrespected me. Rather, I would say "bonjour" as I walked away, leaving them very confused. I didn't allow anything they said to change who I was.

I credit my upbringing that instilled my strong sense of self and pride. I refused to be defined by ignorance. My confidence and attitude, forged by the familiar refrain, were essential elements for dealing with the inevitable difficulty of being different.

My advice to others is to be yourself. Do not allow anyone to change you to what they think you are. Know who you are and be that person.

SHEILA J. WILLIAMS

God opens doors

I was born in St Catherine, Jamaica. I left my country in 1977 and went to the United States. Soon afterwards, I received my documents to come to Canada.

There were several reasons why I left Jamaica. I had been teaching for 16 years, and it was becoming difficult because I was doing more disciplining than teaching. I was not the kids' favourite teacher. Where I went to school to get my diploma, I was not taught the proper way to discipline children. I became very frustrated.

The second reason why I chose to live in Canada was financial. I thought if I were able to come to the United States or Canada, I could earn more money and pay off the mortgage on my house in Jamaica. The corruption in Jamaica also became an issue for me, especially in the 1980s. The thinking was that outside influences were manipulating the people in Jamaica to turn to crime because of all the guns that were coming into the country. Also a lot of kids were not showing up at school because many people were being killed. I witnessed a young man getting killed. I think that was a sign from God to leave Jamaica.

My brother and his family were in Canada already. He actually had tried to sponsor me but Canada had changed its immigration policies on sponsorship and so you couldn't sponsor a family member at that time. That is why I ended up in the US. I know God wanted me to come here because he opened up the doors.

I started working at the library in February 1988. My church supported my family to some extent, because my brother went through a divorce, which was tough on him. I decided then to live on my own. The people at my job were really nice and they helped me learn about the system and more about Canada. The first month I was here I ended up in Ottawa because I met a friend that was very adventurous.

The only thing I dislike about Canada is winter. But I never wanted to go back home. When I retired, everybody expected me to go back home. My best friends are still there, but I didn't have too much family there. I was still hearing stories about the crime back there, so I know I wouldn't have felt safe. I've visited, but I never had the desire to go back and live in Jamaica.

I grew up in Canada, and I would miss all the things I was exposed to here, if I went back. I love the social life in Canada. I was not comfortable living alone in the US and

I didn't like the way they treated Black people. I joined a church in Washington D.C. and made some friends, but it still made me sad to see how Black people were living. The only place I would choose to live in the US is in Atlanta because Blacks are progressing there. I was looking for a job there as well. But in general, I didn't like living in the US. The only time I thought America was progressing was when [Barack] Obama was the President.

I am happy that I came to Canada, where you have the opportunity to live anywhere and feel safe. Canada is also helpful. You also have the opportunity to choose your job. I've always lived in Brampton and I enjoy living here.

I am angry at people who come here and complain about Canada when Canada has so many opportunities such as the healthcare system. If I get sick, I can go to the hospital for free. In the US, I had to get a certificate to see the doctor, which cost me $100, and another $200 for the doctor to sign the certificate. I prayed everyday that I wouldn't get sick because I couldn't afford it.

I am so blessed and grateful to have come to Canada. One thing that always kept me going is always counting my blessings.

CPSIA information can be obtained
at www.ICGtesting.com
Printed in the USA
LVHW031123131219
639947LV00002B/3/P

9 781525 548413